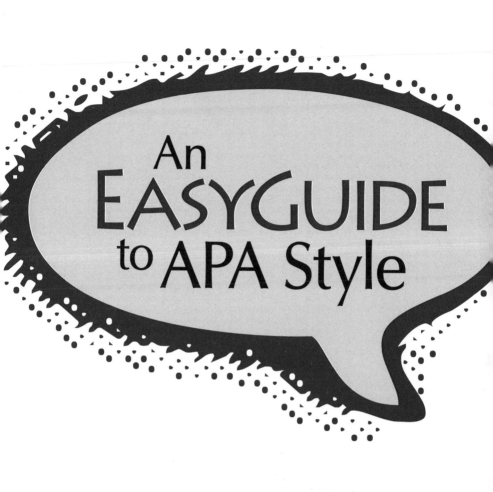

An
EASYGUIDE
to APA Style

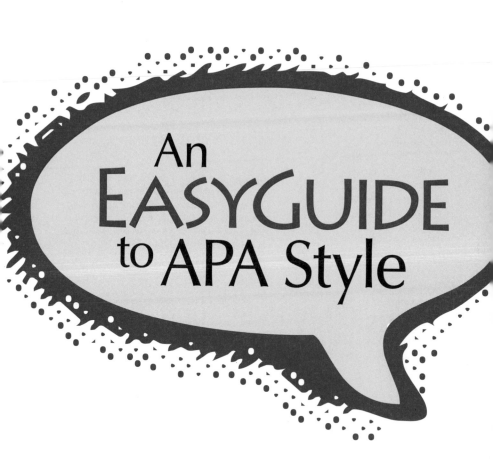

An EASYGUIDE to APA Style

BETH M. SCHWARTZ
Randolph College

R. ERIC LANDRUM
Boise State University

REGAN A. R. GURUNG
University of Wisconsin, Green Bay

$SAGE

Los Angeles | London | New Delhi
Singapore | Washington DC

Los Angeles | London | New Delhi
Singapore | Washington DC

FOR INFORMATION:

SAGE Publications, Inc.
2455 Teller Road
Thousand Oaks, California 91320
E-mail: order@sagepub.com

SAGE Publications Ltd.
1 Oliver's Yard
55 City Road
London EC1Y 1SP
United Kingdom

SAGE Publications India Pvt. Ltd.
B 1/I 1 Mohan Cooperative Industrial Area
Mathura Road, New Delhi 110 044
India

SAGE Publications Asia-Pacific Pte. Ltd.
33 Pekin Street #02-01
Far East Square
Singapore 048763

Acquisitions Editor: Christine Cardone
Editorial Assistant: Sarita Sarak
Production Editor: Astrid Virding
Copy Editor: Linda Gray
Typesetter: C&M Digitals (P) Ltd.
Proofreader: Scott Oney
Indexer: Molly Hall
Cover Designer: Janet Kiesel
Marketing Manager: Liz Thornton
Permissions Editor: Karen Ehrmann

Copyright © 2012 by SAGE Publications, Inc.

Printed in the United States of America

Library of Congress Cataloging-in-Publication Data

Schwartz, Beth M.

An easyguide to APA style / Beth M. Schwartz,
R. Eric Landrum, Regan A. R. Gurung.

p. cm.
Includes bibliographical references and index.

ISBN 978-1-4129-9124-7 (spiral)

1. Psychology—Authorship—Style manuals. 2. Social
sciences—Authorship—Style manuals. I. Landrum,
R. Eric. II. Gurung, Regan A. R. III. Title.

BF76.7.S39 2012 808'.06615—dc22 2010041062

This book is printed on acid-free paper.

11 12 13 14 15 10 9 8 7 6 5 4 3 2 1

Brief Contents

Detailed Contents

SECTION III. WRITING WITH (APA) STYLE: GETTING DOWN TO BUSINESS

Preface

Traveling to a new place can be exciting, but going anywhere for the first time always has its challenges. Whether it is a new city, a new school, or a new job, it takes time to learn the ins and outs of the place, its rules and customs. It is a similar process with learning to write in American Psychological Association (APA) style—that is, learning when to use italics, capitalization, and abbreviations; how to treat numbers; what citations and references should look like; how to set margins; and what headings, tables, and figures should look like as required by the American Psychological Association. At first blush, APA style is almost like a foreign language with its own syntax and grammar, and the manual with all its rules can be as tricky as a labyrinth to navigate for any newcomer. With this *EasyGuide* in hand, you take a great step to making the process of learning how to write papers in APA style much easier. We will help you through the maze of rules, and you will even have (some) fun along the way. Over the years, we have witnessed the many problems our students have when confronting the numerous details involved in creating APA research papers, term papers, or lab reports. We see the frustration our students feel when trying to find the information they need in the APA *Publication Manual* (APA, 2010a) amid the voluminous details that primarily apply to faculty members or graduate students submitting manuscripts for publication. If your needs are similar to our students' needs (i.e., writing papers for class) or even if you are preparing a traditional manuscript for publication, this *EasyGuide* will serve you well. If you are in need of a way to cite and report an uncommon type of reference or statistic, then you may need to also consult the APA *Publication Manual.*

Our Reader-Friendly Approach

We decided to present the essentials of APA style using a more conversational tone in hopes of making this book and the task of learning how to write more enjoyable. We need to state up front that although we address the details of writing papers in APA style and format, *there are times in this book when we do not use APA style and format.* For example, we use contractions when speaking to our readers, although you shouldn't formally write that way. Because this book conforms to the publisher's design, you won't see double-spaced lines with 1″ margins, and you'll notice, for example, that the opening paragraph of each chapter and the first paragraph following a Level 1 heading are not indented. We also flex our funny bones (or muscles) when appropriate. It makes for easier reading, but note that it is not APA style.

With the sample papers illustrating where all the basic rules pertain to their writing, we believe you will be less likely to overlook the different aspects of APA-style writing commonly omitted when first learning this type of writing. We also believe that the list and explanation of the most common errors we've seen over the years will better help you focus on the content of your writing rather than the minutia of APA style and format. The visual table of contents (Chapter 2) and the visual illustrations in the sample paper are unique, illustrating the details not to forget and where in the paper these details apply.

How to Use This Book

In this *EasyGuide,* we've eliminated the search for the basics that can be somewhat time-consuming and confusing. We believe that using this book will save you a significant amount of time, allowing you to focus on writing your paper rather than searching for what you need to know about presenting it in APA style. Here, you'll be able to easily find the information you need, with examples presented visually as well as in the text. We illustrate not only how to write using APA style but also what APA style really looks like when your paper is complete. The sample paper used in the visual table of contents (Chapter 2) lets you see within an actual paper the details you will need to consider when writing in APA style, and the sample indicates where in this book you can find the information needed to learn those details. In addition, that same sample paper is included in Chapter 18 where you'll see the research paper with the details accentuated, but this time the style and format details are explained.

Although we created an organization to the *EasyGuide* that will help you learn the basics in an order we believe makes sense, it is important to remember that each chapter stands alone and you can choose to read the book in whatever order suits your needs best. This may not be the type of book that you read cover to cover but, rather, one you keep as a reference source next to you as you write APA-style papers throughout your undergraduate career. We end the book with a chapter that reviews the most common mistakes we see students encounter when first learning APA style, and we also included a sample paper (with APA errors purposely embedded) so you can test your knowledge. After you have read the book and you want to make sure you are comfortable writing without constantly reaching for the guide, test yourself using the error-filled paper and see if you can find the errors. After all, it is hard to know what you *need* to know if you do not know *what* you know or if what you know is *right*: a little metacognitive self-test as it were. Up for the challenge? Go ahead. To encourage you to use this book while writing, a lay-flat spine was used in hopes of making the writing process easier for you. It's what an EasyGuide is all about.

Similar to the *Publication Manual*, this book does not provide advice about how to write the complete paper. Therefore, we recommend you pair this book with one of the excellent writing psychology texts that we cite in Chapter 19. Although those books describe how to write each section of an APA-style paper, this book focuses on learning the fine points of APA style and format. Both are equally important but with a different goal in mind.

Acknowledgments

A number of individuals made valuable contributions during the development, writing, and editing of this book. We appreciate the learned expertise of our colleagues who helped us shape this book at all steps along the way. For their generous assistance, we are indebted to Stephen F. Davis (Morningside College), Cynthia Noyes (Olivet College), Chris Hakala (Western New England College), Maureen A. McCarthy (Kennesaw State University), Jane S. Halonen (University of West Florida), and Andrew Johnson (Park University). In addition, we are grateful to Randolph A. Smith (Lamar University) for lending his special APA editing expertise to improving our work. At Sage, Christine Cardone was our guide throughout the journey, and without her support, this book would never have been completed. We also appreciate the attention to detail by Sarita Sarak, Linda Gray, and Astrid Virding in helping our efforts come to fruition.

A number of our students were also instrumental in the development and review process, including Jerry Wells from Randolph College, Tiffany Wilhelm from the University of Wisconsin–Green Bay, and Jessica Kesler from Boise State University. When working on any manuscript, family support is crucial, and we all thank our families for helping us maintain our sanity in the midst of deadlines, rewrites, e-mails, and other responsibilities in our lives. Finally, we thank all the students (past, present, and future) who learn to write in APA style and format. The idea for this book came about as we struggled to teach what some consider a foreign language without an appropriate student-friendly resource. Our colleagues at each of our home departments and in the Society for the Teaching of Psychology (www.teachpsych.org) supported us as we worked to create this resource; we are grateful for their support. We hope this *EasyGuide* minimizes or eliminates struggles for faculty and students.

Now, a message from the Sage Legal Department. In a few chapters of this book, we include screenshots of Microsoft Word 2007 so that we can show you what to do in addition to telling you how to do it. Protecting intellectual property rights is important, and failure to do so is akin to plagiarism. So be sure to remember the following:

This book includes screenshots of Microsoft Word 2007 to illustrate the methods and procedures described in this book. Microsoft Word 2007 is a product of the Microsoft Corporation.

We invite you to share the wisdom of your experience with us. We welcome your suggestions for how to make learning APA style even easier, and we welcome your comments as well as suggestions for the second edition of this book. Feel free to e-mail any of us: Beth (bschwartz@randolphcollege.edu), Eric (elandru@boisestate.edu), and Regan (gurungr@uwgb.edu).

About the Authors

Beth M. Schwartz is the William E. and Catherine Ehrman Thoresen '23 Professor of Psychology and assistant dean of the College at Randolph College, in Lynchburg, Virginia. She received a BA at Colby College (Maine) and a PhD in cognitive psychology at the State University of New York at Buffalo. Her scholarship focuses on two areas of interest: (a) children's memory development and how this applies to children's eyewitness reports and (b) the scholarship of teaching and learning/pedagogical research. In addition to numerous professional presentations at conferences, she has published many book chapters and articles in a variety of scholarly journals, including *Law and Human Behaviors* and *Applied Developmental Science*. She has also edited and coauthored books, including *Child Abuse: A Global View* (Schwartz, McCauley, & Epstein, 2001), *Optimizing Teaching and Learning* (Gurung & Schwartz, 2009), and *The Psychology of Teaching: An Empirically Based Guide to Picking, Choosing, & Using Pedagogy* (Schwartz & Gurung, in press). She is a member of the American Psychological Association (APA) and the American Psychological Society (APS) and is a Fellow of Division 2 of APA (Society for the Teaching of Psychology) where she currently serves as Associate Director for Regional Programming. She is an award-winning teacher at Randolph College where she teaches Introduction to Psychology, Research Methods, and the Capstone Course. She received the Award for Outstanding Teaching and Mentoring from the American Psych-Law Society and the Distinguished Faculty Achievement Certificate from the State Council of Higher Education for Virginia.

R. Eric Landrum is a professor of psychology at Boise State University, having received his PhD in cognitive psychology (with an emphasis in quantitative methodology) from Southern Illinois University Carbondale in 1989. His research interests center on the study of educational issues, identifying those conditions that best facilitate student success (broadly defined). He has given more than 250 professional presentations at conferences, published 17 books or book chapters, and published more than 60 professional articles in scholarly, peer-reviewed journals. His work has appeared in journals such as *Teaching of Psychology, College Teaching,* and the *Journal of College Student Development*. He has worked with more than 260 undergraduate research assistants and taught more than 10,000 students in 18 years at Boise State. During the summer of 2008, he led a working group at the National Conference for Undergraduate Education in Psychology concerned with the desired results of an undergraduate psychology education. He is the lead author of *The Psychology Major: Career Options and Strategies for Success* (4th ed., 2009), and he authored *Undergraduate Writing in Psychology: Learning to Tell the Scientific Story* (2008) and *Finding a Job With a Psychology Bachelor's Degree: Expert Advice for Launching Your Career* (2009). He is a member of the American Psychological Association (APA), is a Fellow of Division 2 of APA, and currently serves as Division 2 secretary in addition to Psi Chi vice president of the Rocky Mountain region. He is an award-winning teacher and researcher. At Boise State, he teaches General Psychology, Statistical Methods, Research Methods, and Psychological Measurement.

Regan A. R. Gurung is the Ben J. and Joyce Rosenberg Professor of Human Development and Psychology at the University of Wisconsin, Green Bay (UWGB). He received a BA at Carleton College (Minnesota) and a PhD at the University of Washington. He then spent three years at UCLA. He has published articles in a variety of scholarly journals, including *Psychological Review* and *Teaching of Psychology*. He has a textbook, *Health Psychology: A Cultural Approach* (now in its second edition), and has coauthored/edited six other books: *Exploring Signature Pedagogies: Approaches to Teaching Disciplinary Habits of Mind* (Gurung, Chick, & Haynie, 2009); *Getting Culture* (Gurung & Prieto, 2009); *Optimizing Teaching and Learning* (Gurung & Schwartz, 2009); *The Psychology of Teaching: An Empirically Based Guide to Picking, Choosing, & Using Pedagogy* (Schwartz & Gurung, in press); *Exploring More Signature Pedagogies* (Chick, Haynie, & Gurung, in press); and *Culture & Mental Health* (Eshun & Gurung, 2009). He is a Fellow of both the American Psychological Association (APA) and the American Psychological Society (APS) and a winner of the Founder's Award for Excellence in Teaching as well as the Founder's Award for Scholarship at UWGB; and he was the Carnegie Foundation for the Advancement of Teaching, Wisconsin Professor of the Year (2009). He is currently president of the Society for the Teaching of Psychology (STP, 2011).

SECTION I

Overview

Style Versus Format 1

Why It Matters to Your Audience and Why It Should Matter to You

If you are in college, congratulations—we think you made a good choice! That means you have many papers to write in your future. This book is about helping you become a better writer and helping to build your confidence in your writing ability. In particular, this book is about helping you learn how to write a scientific paper with precision and objectivity, one in which you are able to accurately communicate your ideas, findings, and interpretations using the type of writing style and format published by the American Psychological Association (APA). To help you become APA-style compliant, we use plenty of examples and clever subtitles and any trick we can think of to get your attention to help you learn from the book. In fact, the book is purposely spiral-bound so it can lie flat on your desk next to your computer or in your lap as you are working on your APA papers.

Regardless of whether you are writing a paper as a psychology, sociology, or nursing student, if you are asked to write in APA style, you are asked to do so to help communicate your ideas in writing in a way that will be more easily understood by others in your field. APA style reflects the scientific method in that its goals are precision and objectivity in writing, as well as standardization of style and format. Using APA style helps keep our personal style and eccentricities from affecting our reviewing and reporting of research. It helps maintain the goal of objectivity in science. Specific content is placed within specific sections and in a particular order, allowing the reader to know exactly where to find particular pieces of information about your research. Following APA style and format, you will be able to provide the reader with a convincing argument with clear and concise statements and logical development of your ideas. You will find a greater appreciation for the APA *Publication Manual* once you start reading articles for one of your assignments. Then you will start to notice how helpful it is to have a particular type of writing style and format from one paper to the next, expediting your reading and understanding of the material.

Let us introduce two of the more common terms used when using the APA *Publication Manual* to write your papers: *APA style* and *APA format*. For some assignments, you might be told to "write in APA style"; but others might say "use APA format," or you might just hear "follow the *Publication Manual*." You may be confused by these different instructions. What does it all mean?

What Is the Difference Between APA Style and APA Format?

These terms can be so confusing because there are no clear, set definitions for what they mean. For instance, APA style has been characterized by these writing elements: clarity, literal writing, and brevity (Vipond, 1993). But other types of writing could clearly share these characteristics; for example, wouldn't you want an owner's manual to be clear, literal, and brief? Sure, but owner's manuals are not written in APA style (at least the manuals we have read). For clarity *here* (and for our purposes), we define APA style as *a writing approach that embodies objectivity, credibility of sources, and an evidence-based approach*. For instance, objectivity implies a certain level of detachment and formality; APA style does not typically involve passionate stories written like characters of a play interacting with each other. Objectivity also implies distance and balance in approach. Scientists writing in APA style cover variables and hypotheses and theories (which could involve studying emotion and passion) and how they affect behavior generally. Scientists do not typically write about specific individuals (with the exception of descriptions of case studies). Objectivity in APA style also obligates the writer to avoid biased language and respect the power of language and labels.

APA style necessitates an approach that respects and preserves the chain of evidence and how science builds on previous findings and refines theoretical explanations over time. An example is the citations that an author uses to support claims made in scientific writing. When you see the flow of a sentence or a paragraph interrupted by names and years, this is the author giving credit for ideas—such as exemplified by someone writing about how to optimize teaching and learning (Gurung & Schwartz, 2009)—and giving credit in parentheses. Listing the last names of the authors and the year that the work was published provides evidence for the claim being made by the writer and makes readers aware of the continued refinement of theories from one scientist's work to the next. Giving credit where credit is due also helps avoid plagiarism (see Chapter 5 for details on avoiding plagiarism). Taken together, APA style is one important component of what makes a journal article—and correspondingly, the research presented in it—reflect scientific objectivity.

For our purposes, APA format is what makes a journal article "look" scientific. APA format refers to the precise rules of generating your article, manuscript, or term paper by using the rules set forth in the *Publication Manual*. When we refer to "APA format," we mean the nitty-gritty details about how your written work will appear on paper: the margins, the font, when to use an ampersand (&) and when to use the word *and*. Inserting the correct information in the top 1-inch margin of your paper, when to use numerals (*12*) and when to spell out numbers (*twelve*), how to format tables with only horizontal lines, and how citation styles in the text vary with the number of authors. These details address the appearance of an APA-formatted paper.

An EasyGuide to APA Style is written for students who are learning to write in APA style using APA format. Why not just rely on the "official" book, the sixth edition of the *Publication Manual of the American Psychological Association* (hereafter known as the *PM*; APA, 2010a)? The *PM* is not evil. And if your instructor thinks you should purchase it, then you probably should. But you should know that the *PM* was not written primarily as a guide to help students learn to write better (that is the purpose of *this* book). The *PM* was originally written to provide guidance to researchers on how to submit journal article manuscripts for consideration to be published. However, it is clear that the *PM* has evolved into much more than an instruction set and is now a prescriptive collection of rule (format) and writing advice (style) aimed at facilitating and fostering scientific research. Could you actually use our *EasyGuide* as a replacement to the *PM*? We think so, but be sure to follow the advice of your instructors. After all, they are the ones who are reading, grading, and providing you with feedback. That said, beware the itty-bitty guides to style that are often required for English comp or first-year writing classes. It may be nice to have one book with all the major styles in it, but books like that often do not provide the information needed and therefore are rarely ever a good substitute for the real thing—or better yet, a resource like the one you now hold in your hands.

Here is an analogy to consider when thinking about the *PM*: The 2010 rulebook for Major League Baseball is 240 pages long; knowing the rules to baseball may be important, but just knowing the rules will not make you a better baseball player. However, if you add tons of baseball practice with feedback from knowledgeable sources (such as coaches, older players, books, and videos), you can become a better ballplayer over time. We want this book to be one of those knowledgeable sources that you consult on a regular basis to improve your scientific writing throughout your undergraduate career. Combined, the three of us have taught for a long time and have read and graded more than 10,000 pages of student papers. We take you behind the scenes of writing and point out major common errors so you can avoid them. We have organized this book to make it easy to use to find the information students typically need to know when learning APA style to write papers, which is sometimes not the case with the *PM.*

Why APA Style Anyway?
Wasn't MLA Good Enough?

Odds are that you have already learned some of the rules of at least one other style guide, which may have been MLA (which stands for Modern Language Association). It might have been in high school or even in a college-level English comp class, but you may have used MLA style if you wrote your papers with footnotes, if you had a bibliography or works cited page at the end of your paper, or if you used op. cit. or ibid. in your referencing. The typical MLA method of citing involves listing the author, followed by the page number where information came from in the source (compared with APA style, which uses author followed by year published). So why APA format? Wasn't MLA good enough?

It is hard to know with certainty why MLA style was not adopted for psychological writing. The Modern Language Association was founded in 1883 (MLA, 2009); the American Psychological Association was founded in 1892. However, the first "Instructions" to APA authors was not published until 1929, and the MLA Handbook is now in its seventh edition—formally known as the *MLA Handbook for Writers of Research Papers* (MLA, 2009). So for whatever reason, separate style guides emerged—and there are many more (e.g., Chicago style; American Sociological Association [ASA] style; Turabian style; Modern Humanities Research Association [MHRA] style; and for newspapers, Associated Press [AP] style).

So where did APA style and format come from? In the very first "Instructions in Regard to Preparation of Manuscript" (1929) a six-member panel recommended "a standard of procedure, to which exceptions would doubtless be necessary, but to which reference might be made in cases of doubt" (p. 57). On a less positive (but believable) note, the 1929 "Instructions" noted that "a badly prepared manuscript always suggests uncritical research and slovenly thinking" (p. 58). Whether fair or not, the quality of our writing reflects the quality of our thinking! Good science requires communication, and if we do not communicate well, even the best ideas in the world will not be understood by others (think about the professor who you know is brilliant but has a hard time communicating on a level you can understand). Even though APA format may seem cumbersome to learn, once you are familiar with it, you will feel more comfortable with its conventions. If you have started to read journal articles and papers, you may notice that most, if not all, follow the same organization. The more articles you read, the more thankful you will be that each article is written in the same format and style. It really does make reviewing the literature much easier. We cannot imagine reading a journal article where the Results section appears before the Method section (and that's not because we lack imagination or are geeks). By following (and relying on) APA style and format, we provide readers scaffolding to process the complex ideas and information being presented. Ever watch a movie where the sequence of events is shown out of order (like multiple flashbacks)? Can you tell if something is foreshadowing or background information? Then the movie jumps again. Are we back to the present, or is this a peek into the future? Only once in a while does it work well (check out the movies *Memento* [Todd, Todd, & Nolan, 2000] or David Lynch's *Mulholland Drive* [Edelstein et al., 2001] for a real mind-bending experience). Following a sequence and order provides a framework for understanding what happened, what is happening, and what will happen.

In the Long Run, Attention to Detail Matters (Including APA Style and Format)

As you become familiar with the details of writing in APA style and format, either through using this book alone or using this book with the *PM,* you should keep two important points in mind. First, there will be times when you are frustrated by having to learn a "new" format, when MLA or another style was working just fine before. Although it may be frustrating to learn something new, this is a task that you will repeat hundreds if not thousands of times throughout your work career. It is a task that is part of being an educated person. New procedures will be implemented, a new type of software will be installed, a new gadget will be invented, and your task will be to figure it all out. An inherent love of learning and taking on new challenges are attitudes that will carry you well with your future employers, whoever they may be. So the ability to learn how to write capably in APA style demonstrates a competence you have that others may not share; in fact, you might know fellow students who pick classes with the least amount of writing. If you develop a skill in an area that others systematically avoid, you inevitably make yourself more marketable.

The ability to pay attention to detail, particularly in regard to APA format, can help separate the good from the great. If you can handle both the big picture and the minute details simultaneously, that is a gift. These gifts can be developed with practice. Practice may not make perfect, but practice allows one to get better and closer to perfect. You have to study, you have to learn from mistakes, and you have to be willing to make the mistakes in order to maximize your learning ability; obviously you need to be willing to attempt the task numerous times in order to have these experiences. Paying attention to the details can make the difference between earning an A or a B in a course. You may not like the details or how picky and arbitrary they seem, but knowing the rules (and knowing those occasions when you can break the rules) is invaluable knowledge. Plus, as you will read in this book, those seemingly "picky" rules can be very helpful to practicing robust science.

Just to give you one practical example of how psychologists must also play by these rules, Brewer, Scherzer, Van Raalte, Petitpas, and Andersen (2001) reported that in a survey of journal editors in psychology, 39% of the journal editors responding indicated that they had rejected an article submitted for publication solely because the writing did not adhere to APA style and format. These rules are the same rules that scientists play by, and clearly, the penalties for not following the rules can be harsh for faculty and students alike.

Write for Your Specific Audience: Term Papers Versus Formal Research Papers

Ultimately, we all have to play by the rules. Unfortunately, the rules are often a moving target. Have you heard the variation on the Golden Rule—those who have the gold make the rules? In this case, your audience makes the rules for your writing, and your audience (your instructor) may not always be clear about expectations, which means you have to be. Although there are many excellent, skilled, caring instructors out there (we know many of them and salute them all), not all pay as much attention to the assignment design as they could. For example, an instructor may give a writing assignment, like the one in the following box, thinking that the instructions are perfectly clear. But see how many questions we have after reading the "assignment."

Before class next week, I want you to pick a topic in psychology and write a research paper about your topic. Be sure to use evidence to support your position. Make sure you complete the following:

1. Write in APA format.

2. Your paper must be 5–7 pages in length.

3. To save paper, use single-spacing.

4. Use reference citations in the text of your paper to support any claims that you make.

The paper is due on Thursday, and here it is Wednesday night; you sit down to write your paper—no problem. Take a closer look at this assignment; it is wide open and does not provide enough detail so that you can be confident that you know what your audience (your instructor) wants. The instruction "write in APA format" is vague at best, especially because it is contradicted by the third point in the assignment; APA format uses double-spacing in the text. Does this instructor want a title page? An abstract (probably not)? A references page? Do the title page and the references page "count" in the 5- to 7-page assignment? Are direct quotations OK? Are a minimum number of references required? Can you use all kinds of reference materials or just refereed journal articles?

First an important point: We hope you know that it pays to start writing earlier. Not only would you have more time to get clarification on the assignment; you would have time to write more than one draft, something that contributes to higher quality papers (Landrum, 2008). Additionally, research shows that students who start assignments earlier do better in class (Gurung, 2009).

A basic tenet of any type of writing is this: Write for your audience. In most cases now, your audience is your instructor. So you need to know what your instructor wants, even if the instructor thinks he or she is being clear in the instructions. You need to know the questions to ask so that you can get the answers you need to succeed. This book will help you identify which questions to ask, and when you get the answers, we will give you specific tips on how to do well on the major parts of your writing assignments, whether they are term papers or research papers.

What is the difference between a term paper and a research paper, and why would it matter? Generally, a term paper may be a review of a topic using research and citations, but a term paper could also be an opinion paper about a particular topic. A research paper, especially in psychology (as in an experimental paper), is typically more scripted than a term paper. In a research paper, you are likely to have specific subsections, such as a Method section and a Results section, and many other details to attend to. A research paper is likely to employ APA style and most, if not all, components of APA format. A term paper could adhere to these same characteristics, but not necessarily so. Confused? Make sure you ask the instructor specifically what he or she wants from the paper. Instructors may think they are being clear, but just saying "APA format" might only mean 1-inch margins, whereas anything else you do is fine. Even though APA style and format provide particulars about how to write your paper, what you will discover is that different instructors have different expectations about style and format; attention to detail will be of ultimate importance to some, or others may not care at all. You cannot use a "one-size-fits-all" approach and expect to be consistently successful in your coursework. You may need to change your writing approach to fit both the assignment and the instructor; in fact, your instructor's expectations during a semester may change as well (we know . . . that can be frustrating). Do not be shy. Ask questions. If you are brave, point out inconsistencies, pay attention to details, and work to meet the needs of your audience. If you can conquer these lessons as an undergraduate, these skills and abilities will serve you well beyond graduation.

Your Visual Table of Contents QuickFinder 2

Have you ever had the challenge of looking up a word in the dictionary that you weren't sure you knew how to spell? In a similar vein, you might not know you need help in formatting your running head if you don't know what a running head is. You can't search for how to include a part of your paper or how to follow a certain rule if you don't even know that part of the paper or that rule exists. Consequently, we designed a "visual table of contents" for you in this chapter, where we show you a complete sample research paper, and rather than give you tips about it and suggestions for avoiding mistakes (which we will do in Chapter 19), in this chapter, we use the sample paper as a visual organizer. Not sure how to cite a reference in text? Find an example of what you are trying to do in the sample paper, and then follow the QuickFinder guide bubbles that will point you to the chapter and page in this book where you can find help.

By the way, this is a real student paper. Parts of it have been modified from the original, but this is meant to be a realistic example of student work. Is it a perfect paper? No (and Jessica is OK with that). Will you be able to find errors or mistakes in the paper? Probably. We use this paper as a visual guide, *not* as an exemplar of perfection. The point is not to look for errors, but to easily identify where in this guide we discuss the different parts of a paper. So, do not use this paper as a model of exactly what to do (because as we said there are errors here), but instead use it as a way to easily find what you want to learn about. Some of our QuickFinder bubbles point at mistakes, but most are positioned just to draw your attention to different parts of a paper and what needs to be considered before you turn in a paper. If you want to use this sample paper to test your knowledge of APA style and format feel free to mark up the errors and see if you can correct them once you have mastered this guide.

Most of the items included in the QuickFinder bubbles you will also find in the table of contents at the beginning of this book. We decided to include this visual table of contents in part for those of us who prefer and are more comfortable seeing content illustrated visually. Note we did *not* say "for the visual learners." Although early research suggested that some folks are visual learners and created the belief that there are different types of learning styles, such as auditory, kinesthetic (involving physical movement), tactile (hands-on, such as in a laboratory setting), and so on (Reid, 1984), more recent evidence indicates that this notion seems to be a myth with little empirical support (Pashler, McDaniel, Rohrer, & Bjork, 2008). That being said, we like the idea of helping you identify APA-style details using different mechanisms, including a sample paper with a visual table of contents. So if you are trying to find information that you think is or should be in this book, you can try the traditional table of contents at the front of the book, the index at the back of the book, and the visual table of contents here in this chapter, with the QuickFinder guides.

The Sample Paper With Content and Page Numbers

Running head: THE INTERNET AND ACADEMICS   1

> **Your Running Hea**
> Inside the top 1-inch m
> See Ch. 12, p. 108
> Formatting with Wor
> See Ch. 14, p. 129

> **Order of Pages**
> Title page always first
> See Ch. 12, p. 107

Problematic Internet Use and the Effect on Academic Performance

Jessica T. Kesler

Boise State University

> **Line Spacing**
> Double-space throughout,
> even on the title page
> See Ch. 12, p. 107

> **Setting the Margins**
> **All Pages**
> Word step-by-step
> instructions
> See Ch. 14, p. 126

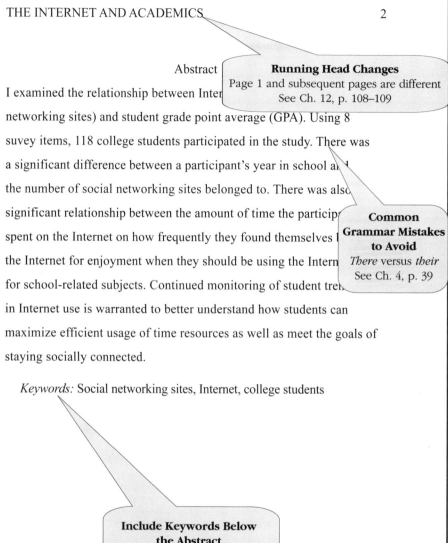

THE INTERNET AND ACADEMICS 2

Abstract

Running Head Changes
Page 1 and subsequent pages are different
See Ch. 12, p. 108–109

I examined the relationship between Inter networking sites) and student grade point average (GPA). Using 8 suvey items, 118 college students participated in the study. There was a significant difference between a participant's year in school a the number of social networking sites belonged to. There was als significant relationship between the amount of time the particip spent on the Internet on how frequently they found themselves the Internet for enjoyment when they should be using the Intern for school-related subjects. Continued monitoring of student tre in Internet use is warranted to better understand how students can maximize efficient usage of time resources as well as meet the goals of staying socially connected.

**Common
Grammar Mistakes
to Avoid**
There versus *their*
See Ch. 4, p. 39

Keywords: Social networking sites, Internet, college students

**Include Keywords Below
the Abstract**
Format rules for keywords
See Ch. 19, p. 173

> **Center the Title**
> Instructions for Word
> See Ch. 14, p. 133

3

> **Use Your Tools**
> Use spell-checker and grammar
> check. See Ch. 18, p. 159

...MICS

...e Effect on Academic Performance

College institutions worldwide have come into the twenty-first
century by making the Internet available in many areas around their
campuses. In fact, the Internet is so accessible that students may choose
to surf the Internet over studying, potentially sacrifi...

> **Avoid Plagiarism**
> Cite direct quotations
> properly
> See Ch. 5, p. 46

for a few extra moments of entertainment. Although
available a wealth of knowledge that students can us
presents opportunities to distract users from being prod...   ...Kraut,
Patterson, & Lundmark, 1998). Although the Inter...   ...considered a good
resource by many, too much of anything may ...   ...armful. According to

> **Line and Paragraph Spacing**
> Consistency matters
> throughout
> See Ch. 14, p. 127

...Buzlu (2007), healthy Intern... ...se is "use of the Internet for
...d purpose in a reasonab... amount of time without cognitive
...discomfort" (p. 768). By letting one's Internet use effect
...uccess, you may no longer have a grasp healthy Internet use
(Oz... ...& Buzlu, 2007).

Researchers at Ohio Siale University completed a pilot
study on the effects of social networking sites (specifically Facebook)

> **Follow In-Text Citation Rules**
> In parentheses, use &,
> not *and*
> See Ch. 7, p. 61

...ance, and concluded that college students who use
...orking site Facebook spend less time studying
...oint averages (GPA) than their peers who have
...urthermore, the typical Facebook user has a GPA
of about 3.0 to... ...whereas non-Facebook users had GPAs between 3.5
and 4.0 (Karpinski & Duberstein, 2009). The differences in GPA could be
linked to the number of hours a week spent studying—5 hours for users,
compared to 11 to 15 hours per week for nonusers. But the authors of this

THE INTERNET AND ACADEMICS   4

study did not draw the conclusion that using social networking sites leads

to lower grades, and that possibly other factors like personality, could

link Facebook usage and lower GPA. Pempek, Yermolayeva, and Calvert

(2009) stated "it may he that if it wasn't for Facebook, some students

would still find other ways to avoid studying, and would still get lower

grades. But perhaps the lower GPAs could actually be because students

are spending too much time socializing online" (p. 236).

The effects of using the Internet too much can range

effects, such as time management issues and social isolati

severe effects like cravings, sleep disturbance, depression,

withdrawal symptoms in association with excessive time o

et al., 1998). Although some of these symptoms appear simila

tʰ se of a drug or alcohol addiction, according to Scherer (1997), one

not be physiologically addicted to the Internet the way one might

drugs and alcohol, but using the Internet excessively can lead to

ar dependent behavior and cravings. Kubey, Lavin, and Barrows

) found that 13% of college students have Internet dependency

ems. There is also a relationship between online procrastination

and problematic Internet use. Studying these two concepts addresses the

potential lack of self-control over the time spent on the Internet

and the lack of ability to acknowledge the distraction and

entertainment the Internet can provide. In a study by Thatcher,

Wretschko, and Fridjhon (2008), these researchers found a strong

correlation between problematic Internet use and procrastination

because the Internet provides people with a means of stress relief and

entertainment, making procrastination easy, particularly since

> **Avoid Plagiarism**
> Paraphrase in your
> own words
> See Ch. 5, p. 48

> n-Text
> ations,
> ultiple
> uthors
> the rules
> sing *et al.*
> h. 7, p. 62

THE INTERNET AND ACADEMICS   5

individuals possess the ability to look engaged, although potentially not academically engaged at all.

The goal of my study is to partially replicate the previous pilot from Ohio State University (Karpinski & Duberstein, 2009), and expand upon the knowledge about the impact of Internet usage on academic performance, possibly because of use of the Internet for procrastination. Participants self-selected from a pool of Boise State University general psychology students who were then asked to complete a survey regarding their Internet usage habits and academic progress. I hypothesize that the more time a student spends using the Internet. the lower the student's GPA. I also hypothesize that the more social netw**Avoid Passive Voice** Active voice here preferred over "It was hypothesized that..." See Ch. 3, p. 31 lower that person's GPA. The final hypothesi time a person spends on the Internet, the more often they would be using the Internet for fun when they should be using the Inter academics.

> **Avoid Gender-Biased Language**
> Use *their* to avoid *he/she*
> See Ch. 6, p. 54

> **Avoid Passive Voice**
> Active voice here preferred over "It was hypothesized that..."
> See Ch. 3, p. 31

> **Formatting Method Secti**
> Boldfaced headings, centered or r
> See Ch. 8, p.

Method

Participants

> **Participants or Subjects**
> See Ch. 8, p. 69

ere 118 participants in this study; 60 women, 47 men, pants not reporting sex. Participants were general psychology students who enrolled for participation using the web-based program Experimetrix. The average age was 20.84 (SD - 6.04). The sample consisted of 75 freshmen, 26 sophomores, 5 juniors, 2 seniors, and 10 participants who did not report year in school. Participants in general psychology were rewarded with course credit for their participation.

Materials or Apparatus
What to include
See Ch. 8, p. 71

D ACADEMICS   6

Materials

Participants responded to eight questions relating to their Internet use and their academic success. I created these questions, and the items were pilot tested prior to being administered to the participants. Please see Table 1 for a list of questions presented to participants by this study, including overall means and standard deviations.

Procedure

The eight questions used in this study were part of a l~~~ ~~~~~~~~~

survey that consisted of 234 total questions. Participants we

groups and given 50 ~~min to complete~~

**Rules for Units
of Measure**
Time abbreviations
See Ch. 11, p. 98

within 45 min. After completing the survey, participants were debriefed, thanked for their participation, and given course credit toward research exposure requirements.

Results

In reference to the first hypothesis predicting that the more time a student spends on the Internet, the lower the grade point average (GPA), I conducted a correlation between answers to the item "how many hours do you use the Internet during an average week (for both academic and entertainment purposes)" (answered on an interval/ratio scale) and answers to the item "what is your current GPA" (answered on a scale f~~~~ ~~~~~~~~

There was a statistically significant negative correlation b

the survey items, $r(59) = .28, p$

**Properly Present
Statistical Symbols**
Know what the symbols mean
See Ch. 9, p. 79–80

The second hypothesis is that the more social networking sites one belongs to, the lower the GPA., regardless of gender and year in school.

THE INTERNET AND ACADEMICS   7

Answers to the item "how many social networking sites do you

belong to, i.e., MySpace, Facebook, Twitter" were correlated with

answers to the GPA question. There is not a significa~~nt~~

between number of subscribed social networking si

$r(71) = -.01, p = .936.$

> **Treat Each Number as a Separate Word**
> Spaces around the equals
> See Ch. 9, p. 81

The third hypothesis is that the more time a person uses the

Internet, that time is spent more for fun that for academic purposes. I

explored Internet usage using answers to two survey questions: "how

ocial networking sites do you belong to (i.e., MySpace, Facebook,

, etc." (answered on an interval ratio) ad "how many hours do

the Internet during an average week (for both academic and

nment purposes" (answered on an interval/ratio scale). The

s to these two time/frequency measures were both correlated with

> **Present Lists With Proper Format**
> Seriation and enumeration
> See Ch. 15, p. 145

th nswers to these two Likert-type agreement ($1 = $ *strongly disagree*

$5 = $ *strongly agree*) items: (1) I find that my use of the Internet interfe

with my ability to get good grades, and (2) I believe that my Internet use ca

me to procrastinate on my studies. Number of social networking sites was

not significantly correlated with answers to the item "I find that my use

of the Internet interferes with my ability to get good grades, $r(100) = .13,$

$p = .196.$ Number of social networking sites was significantly positives

c elated with answers to the item "I believe that the Internet causes

procrastinate on my studies," $r(99) = .22, p = .028.$ Time on the

t was significantly positively correlated with answers to the item

that my use of the Internet interferes with my ability to get good

," $r(83) = .24, p = .031.$ Time on the Internet was not significantly

correlated with answers to the item "I believe that my Internet use causes

me to procrastinate on my studies, $r(79) = .15, p = .179.$

> **Formatt Numbe**
> When to in
> a leading
> See Ch.
> p. 101

> **Number of Decimal Places**
> When the rules change
> See Ch. 11, p. 101–102

THE INTERNET AND ACADEMICS   8

> **Multiple Citations Within Parentheses**
> Separate with semicolon
> See Ch. 7, p. 63

> **Avoid Biased Language**
> Put people first
> ("students who value")
> See Ch. 6, p. 50

> **Common Grammar Mistakes to Avoid**
> *Than* versus *then*
> See Ch. 4, p. 40

> **Subject-Verb Agreement**
> Number...does
> See Ch. 3, p. 30

Students self-report that the more time they spend on the Internet, the lower their GPA will be. This finding is in concert with previous research (e.g., Karpinski &, Duberstein, 2009; Pempek, et al., 2009). Although this is a cause and effect result, students who value their GPA (as many do) should be aware of this statistical relationship. Although time on the Internet was significantly correlated with GPA, the number of social networking sites belonged to was not significantly correlated to GPA. Students who use the Internet for far more than just social networking, the number of social networking sites subscribed to was not related to GPA (but overall time on the Internet correlated negatively with GPA). Further hypotheses attempted to tease apart the precise nature of this relationship.

Through a series of four correlations. I explored the relationship between the time and number of sites items with two additional survey items about student self-report that the use of the Internet interferes with my ability to get good grades, and that use of the Internet causes procrastination. Interestingly, the number of social networking sites does correlate positively with the belief that the Internet causes procrastination, but time on the Internet does interfere with my ability to get good grades. Although students do acknowledge a link between increased Internet time and lower GPA/poorer grades, they do not limit this perception to the use of social networking sites. Rather, students report their increased use of social networking sites as a mechanism for procrastination, but not relating to grades.

These findings coincide with the Ohio State University pilot study hypothesis that the average student who did not have Facebook spent 11 to 15 hours studying, whereas a student with Facebook spent only *5* hours

THE INTERNET AND ACADEMICS 9

Use Commonly Confused Words Properly
Affect versus *effect*
See Ch. 3, p. 28

Karpinski & Duberstein, 2009). So it is possible that those ss than 5 hours online may spend more time studying, and ent between 21-25 hours on the Internet were studying very little. oal of this study was not to a complete replication of Karpinski and Dube in (2009), but to expand upon the idea that involvement iti any social tworking site (not just Facebook) has an effect on participant GPA. was unable to replicate the findings demonstrating social networking's effect on GPA, but I did find a significant correlation between the number of social networking sites a participant belonged to and their level of procrastination. One possible danger here for students

Hyphenation and Spelling
See *Webster's* for questions about spelling and hyphenation
See Ch. 12, pp. 111–114

Detailed Punctuatio and Spacing Rules
Tend to the details
See Ch. 16, p. 151–1

nay not realize that too much procrastination (that is, too etworking) may ultimately impact grades a report that they believe no relationship exist orted by Thatcher et al, (2008) coincide wi s found in this study between the number of hours cipant spent e Internet and how often the participant found selves browsing Internet for enjoyment instead of academ. The study conducted b Thatcher, et al. (2008) examined the i a that the Internet provides peop with a means of procrastination. The relationship between online p crastination and problematic Internet use deals with the issue of lack of self control over time spent on the Internet and the lack acknowledgment of the distraction the Internet can provide (Thatcher, et al., 2008).

The results of this study confirm in a speculative manner that Internet usage does vary between students, and that more social networking and more time spent social networking can detract from school-related studies

THE INTERNET AND ACADEMICS   10

and grades. The results of such studies could not only have an impact in
the academic world, but also in other areas where Internet use may be
present, such as in the workplace. The need for a greater understanding
of the effects of Internet use, as well as possible strategies to avoid
the misuse of the Internet, should be a continuing focus of study. For
example, perhaps procrastination early in an assignment timeline
has little to no effect on assignment performance, but procrastination
prior to the assignment due date has more substantial effects.
Understanding when Internet use for pleasure and social networking is
a key determination that students must make in order to also achieve
academic goals.

The limitations of this study were the limited number of
questions, as well as some of the written questions. It would be
advantageous to continue studies over time to see if changes in GPA
are sensitive to the time constraints (or lack thereof) regarding Internet
usage. The Internet is a very present technology in society. With
over half of the United States population with home Internet access
(U.S. Census Bureau, 2007), the Internet makes available a wealth of
can use, but it also poses a threat to a person's
al., 1998). It is clear from experience and from
data gathered during the course of this study that the use of social
networking sites the amount of time spent may be detrimental
to student study habits. It would be of great benefit to the general
population to understand the negative effects of social networking
sites and problematic Internet use, so that individuals may prosper
from appropriate usage.

Correct Punctuation Use
Suggestions for commas
See Ch. 16, p. 152

Insert a Page Break
Learn how and when
you need to
See Ch. 14, p. 139

Reference for a Conference Presentation
Include year and month
See Ch. 10, p. 90

THE INTERNET AND ACADEMICS   11

Ref nces

Karpinski, A., & Duberstein, A. (2009, April). A *description of Facebook use and academic performance among undergraduate and graduate students.* Presented at the annual meeting of the American Educational Research Association, San Diego, CA.

Many Details in a Journal Article Reference
Tend to be details
See Ch. 10,

Kraut, R., Patterson, M., & Lundmark, V. (1998). Internet paradox: A social technology that reduces social involvement and psychological well-being? *American Psychologist, 53,* 1017-1031. doi:10.1037/0003-066X.53.9.1017

Kubey, R. W., Lavin, M. J., & Barrows, J. R. (2001). Internet use and collegiate academic performance decrements: Early findings. *Journal of Communication, 51,* 366-382. doi:10.1111/j.460-2466.2001.tb02K85.x

Ozean, N. K., & Buzlu, S. (2007). Internet use and its relation with the psychosocial situation for a sample of university students. *CyberPsychology and Behavior, 10,* 767-772. doi:10.1089/cpb.2007.9953

Pempek, T., Yermolayeva, Y., & Calvert, S. (2009). College students' social networking experiences on Facebook. *Journal of Applied Developmental Psychology. 30,* 227-23 appdev.2008.12.010

Capitalization Rules
May not be what you are used
See Ch. 12, p. 114

Scherer, K. (1997). College life on-line: Healthy and use. *Journal of College Student Development, 38,*   65.

Thatcher. A., Wretschko, G., & Fridjhon, P. (200). Online flow experience, problematic Internet use and Internet procrastination. *Computers in Human Behavior, 24,* 2236-2254. doi: 10.l016/j.chh.2007.10.008

THE INTERNET AND ACADEMICS   12

U.S. Census Bureau. (2007). *Internet use triples in decades, Census*

Bureau reports. Retrieved from http://www.census.gov/PressRelease/

www/releases/archives/communication_ industries/ 013849.html

mat References With a
Hanging Indent
Use a Word shortcut
See Ch. 10, p. 92
ep-by-step instructions
See Ch. 14, p. 134

Why All These APA Formatting Rules?
What is the point? Why not MLA?
See Ch. 1, p. 6

What About the Paper's Content
This same paper, with content feedback
See Ch. 19, pp. 173–184

The Most Common Mistakes to Avoid
Your presubmission checklist
See Ch. 20, pp. 187–190

THE INTERNET AND ACADEMICS 13

Table 1

Survey Items with Means (M) *and Standard Deviations* (SD)

Survey Item	M	S D
1. find that my use of the Internet interferes my ability to get good grades.	2.61	1.05
2. Internet use causes me to studies.	3.58	1.05
3. How frequently do you find yourself browsing the Internet for fun when you should be using the Internet for school-related subjects?	1.57	.74
4. How many hours do you use the Internet during an average week (for both academic and entertainment purposes)?	14.96	12.25
5. How many social networking sites do you belong to (i.e., MySpace, Facebook, Twitter)?	1.85	1.24
6. What is your current GPA?	3.28	.54

Notes. Item 1 and 2 were answered using a Likert-type agreement scale, with 1 = *strongly disagree* to 5 = *strongly agree.* Item 3 was answered using a frequency scale, with 0 = *never* to 3 = *always.* Items 4, 5 and 6 were fill-in-the-blank questions.

Creating Tables in MS Word
Use the tables function for greater flexibility
See Ch. 14, p. 136

The Table Note
Specific rules for table notes
See Ch. 13, p. 121

SECTION II

Writing With (APA) Style: Big Picture Items

Bare-Bones Fundamentals 3

General Writing Tips
Specific to APA Style

It would be difficult to teach (or reteach) the complexity of how to write within one book such as this one. However, because of our experience in teaching students how to write (specifically, how to write using APA style and format), we offer some targeted advice about the most common mistakes we see in our students' writing and the actions to take to help prevent those mistakes in the future. This way, you benefit from the past mistakes of others. It's almost no pain, but with gain.

Clear and Succinct Writing

As with any type or genre of writing, it takes both time and practice to get good at it and build your confidence. Scientific writing has its own voice, with the appropriate levels of formality, detachment, and objectivity. Even with these style rules, scientific writing does not have to be boring. In fact, the better journal articles in psychology are written to tell a good story. Even though the language may not use a conversational tone, this decision is a purposeful one to be clear and concise. Clear communication is the primary objective—to present ideas precisely, with logic and a smooth flow from idea to idea (Knight & Ingersoll, 1996).

In some college writing, such as composing a term paper or answering an essay question on an exam, you might tend to go on and on, hoping the instructor "finds" the right answer buried somewhere in your prose. Scientific writing does not share that same strategy. You should always strive to be succinct—concise and to the point—and not throw in everything except the kitchen sink. As readers, we appreciate the courtesy of authors who write in this manner; the author does not waste our time with unnecessary words or ideas to clutter the central message. However, as writers, it takes time and practice to acquire this skill; we've designed this book to help you improve as a succinct writer. Knight and Ingersoll (1996) captured the essence of this approach:

> Vigorous writing is concise and direct. A sentence should contain no unnecessary words and a paragraph no unnecessary sentences. This does not mean that all sentences and paragraphs should be short or lacking in detail, but that every word is purposeful. (p. 210)

Commonly Confused Words in Psychology

Like other disciplines, psychology has its own terminology and definitions. Your topic-specific textbooks (such as your introductory psychology textbook, your cognitive psychology textbook, etc.) introduce you to the specific, technical terms. But even in your own writing about psychology, common words are frequently confused; sometimes this is due to a psychological "spin" placed on those words. Following is a brief listing of commonly confused words, with definitions designed to clear up the confusion (with some assistance from www .dictionary.com).

advice/advise

  advice: *noun,* an opinion given, such as a recommended action

  advise: *verb,* to give counsel to, information, or notice

affect/effect

  affect: *verb,* to act on or produce a change in; *noun,* feeling or emotion

  effect: *noun,* a result or consequence; *verb,* to bring about

allusion/illusion

  allusion: *noun,* the incidental mentioning or casual referral

  illusion: *noun,* a type of deception or false impression of reality

cite/site/sight

  cite: *verb,* to quote (typically) an authority, to mention as proof

  site: *noun,* the position or location of an item to be located; *verb,* to put into position or locate

  sight: *noun,* vision, the perception of objects with your eyes; *verb,* to see or notice or observe

conscience/conscious

> conscience: *noun,* one's inner sense of right and wrong; ethical, moral principles
>
> conscious: *adjective,* one's own awareness of thoughts, sensations, existence

council/counsel

> council: *noun,* an assembly of individuals selected to provide consultation or advice
>
> counsel: *noun,* advice given to direct the conduct of someone else; *verb,* to advise or give advice

data/datum

> data: *noun, plural form,* individual facts, statistics, or items of information
>
> datum: *noun,* singular form of data for one number or a single case

elicit/illicit

> elicit: *verb,* to extract, bring out, or evoke
>
> illicit: *adjective,* unlawful, not legally permitted or authorized

lay/lie

> lay: *verb,* to place or to put an object at rest, or set down
>
> lie: *verb,* to be in a horizontal position, recline, to rest, remain, to be situated; to spread a falsehood; *noun,* a false statement made with intention to deceive, a falsehood

personal/personnel

> personal: *adjective,* pertaining to one individual, private
>
> personnel: *noun,* the collection of individuals employed in an organization

precede/proceed

> precede: *verb,* to go before, to introduce something preliminary
>
> proceed: *verb,* to move or go forward, to carry on or continue an action; *noun,* the total amount derived from a sale or transaction

principal/principle

> principal: *adjective,* highest rank of importance or value; *noun,* a chief or head or director
>
> principle: *noun,* fundamental or general law or truth from which other truths are derived

respectfully/respectively

> respectfully: *adverb,* showing politeness or deference
>
> respectively: *adverb,* in the precise order given, sequentially

then/than

> then: *adverb,* at that time, next in order of time, in that case; *noun,* that time; *adjective,* existing or acting (e.g., "the then president")

> than: *conjunction,* used to show unequal comparison (e.g., "colder than yesterday"), used to show difference or diversity; *preposition,* to connect two nouns (e.g., "this is better than that")

Subject-Verb Agreement

The idea of subject-verb agreement may seem simple at first, but the rules get complicated quickly. The subject of a sentence is typically the source of action in a sentence, and often, the subject appears before of the verb. The subject of a sentence can be singular or plural, and thus the verb used has to "agree" with the singularity or plurality of the subject (EzineArticles.com, 2009a). Consider the sentence "I love you." *I* is the subject, which is to the left of the verb *love,* and the object of the sentence (i.e., the one who receives love) is *you* (EzineArticles.com, 2009b). The most common subject-verb error we come across in our students' papers involves a sentence about the data collected for an experiment. *Data* is a plural noun and therefore should always be followed by the verb *are* rather than *is* (or *were* rather than *was* for the past tense).

> The data were collected when all 20 participants were seated in the laboratory.

Here are some general tips to help you figure out the *basic* rules of subject-verb agreement (About.com, n.d.; EzineArticles.com, 2009a), followed by some practice sentences to see if you can identify errors (not every sample sentence has an error, however).

1. Add an *s* to the verb if the subject is a singular noun (a word that names one person, place, or thing).

   A good research idea **takes** time to develop.

2. Add an *s* to the verb if the subject is any one of the third-person singular pronouns: *he, she, it, this, that.*

   She **writes** well and should have her work published.

3. Do not add an *s* to the verb if the subject is the pronoun *I, you, we,* or *they.*

   You **create** a new data file for each online survey.

4. Do not add an *s* to the verb if two subjects are joined by *and.*

   Utah and Idaho **compete** for similar grant projects.

5. *Everybody* is singular and uses a singular verb (as do *anybody, no one, somebody, nobody, each, either,* and *neither*).

Everybody **is** invited to the colloquium on Thursday afternoon.

Active Voice Versus Passive Voice in APA Style

For many native English speakers, subject-verb agreement is only an occasional problem, and by practicing and attending to the rules, these types of errors can be minimized or eliminated. However, depending on your prior writing experience, slipping into passive voice can be natural. Additionally, some students think that writing by using passive voice is more "scientific sounding," and makes the text seem more detached and objective, as scientific writing often strives to be. Unfortunately, passive voice makes writing more muddled, often placing the subject of the sentence after the verb. We generally prefer—and understand better—when we follow the subject-verb-object pattern in a sentence. Clarity is key, and writing in active voice typically provides the best shot at clear communications.

So what is the difference between "active voice" and "passive voice"? The structure of an active voice sentence tends to follow the pattern performer (subject)→verb→receiver (object). The active voice indicates stronger writing because the sentence gives credit to who is performing the action; in other words, the active voice focuses on the performer of the action. Using the active voice is an indicator of clear and vigorous writing, and the active voice is preferred in most academic writing (BioMedical Editor, 2009; DailyWritingTips.com, n.d.; Knight & Ingersoll, 1996; PlainLanguage.gov, n.d.). Using passive voice (in which the pattern is receiver→verb→perfomer, with the performer often not named) is sometimes a difficult habit to break for some educators, because the tradition at one time preferred a passive voice–third-person approach because it implied a sense of detachment and objectivity (BioMedical Editor, 2009; Knight & Ingersoll, 1996). A sentence written in passive voice emphasizes the receiver of the action and not the subject performing the action. Unfortunately, passive voice often adds confusion to understanding the sentence, particularly the subject of the sentence. Here are some examples of **active** voice sentences:

My students completed the survey before time elapsed.

I analyzed possible sex differences using an independent means *t* test.

We recruited students from introductory psychology to participate in this research project.

I prefer using Word on a PC rather than on a Mac.

As you can see, all these sentences are straightforward and relatively easy to understand. Consider these passive sentences and their active counterparts (PlainLanguage.gov, n.d.):

Passive: My car was driven to work. **Active:** I drove my car to work.

Passive: Breakfast was eaten by me this morning. **Active:** I ate breakfast this morning.

It may seem absurd that anyone would purposely use passive voice, but writers (often new to scientific writing) slip into passive voice by accident (and there are times when passive voice is preferred; see the following examples). Knight and Ingersoll (1996, p. 212) expressed opinions a bit stronger about using passive voice, calling it "dry, dull, rigid, pompous, ambiguous, weak, evasive, convoluting, tentative, timid, sluggish, amateurish"—you get the picture. Notice how easily you can slip into passive voice by accident:

The data were analyzed using SPSS. (The subject is not named: Who used SPSS to analyze the data?)

This conclusion was reached by the researchers in the study. (Notice the pattern: The object—*conclusion*—precedes the verb, and the subject—*researchers*—follows the verb.)

Although manic depression was identified in some of the participants, the drug treatment was beneficial for all participants in the study. (The first part of the sentence—"manic depression was identified"—is passive; the second part—"drug treatment was beneficial"—is not passive because the subject precedes the verb.)

You can imagine reading each of these three sentences in a journal article, yet all three are written in passive voice. So when would you use passive voice? Passive voice is useful when you want to emphasize the receiver (or object) of the action (BioMedical Editor, 2009). That is, passive voice is appropriate when you are writing a sentence and you do not know the performer of the action or when the performer of the action is unimportant (PlainLanguage.gov, n.d.). For instance, passive voice may be more appropriate when writing the Method section of a manuscript, because the Method section is likely to focus on objects such as materials and procedures (APA, 2010a). An excellent tip to help you find possible instances of your inadvertent passive voice use is to check your file for some form of the verb "to be"—including *is, are, was,* or *were* (DailyWritingTips .com, n.d.; Knight & Ingersoll, 1996). Notice in the examples, the "to be" verb is included with an additional verb in each passive voice sentence but not in the active voice sentences. Before you hand in a paper, you might use your *Find* feature in Word 2007 under the *Home→Editing* tab (use *Find* on the *Edit* menu in Word 2003, or in either version of word, just press Ctrl+F to get the *Find what* box) and find all the occurrences of *is, are, was,* and *were* to check for passive voice sentences, keeping in mind that passive voice includes these "to be" verbs with another verb that follows (e.g., "Surveys *were collected* by the research assistants").

This notion of proofreading your work before you turn it in brings up another vital practice that you need to use if you want to improve your writing skills: You must learn to write for your audience, and in college, that will typically mean writing for your professors. They may ask for deviations from APA style and APA format, and that is OK. Remember, they are the folks who are grading your work. So if they prefer more of passive voice in scientific writing, follow that advice over the course of the class, but know that the *PM* indicates a preference for the active voice (Section 3.18). In Chapter 18, we provide details on how to best proofread your papers.

Like everything else regarding writing, we get better with practice. So we close this chapter with some sentences that you might encounter in scientific writing; your task is to rewrite them in the active voice. Your rewrites do not need to match perfectly, but take note of the different methods you can use to rewrite into the active voice by putting the "doer" of the action first, followed by the verb, and ending with the object or receiver of the action. This practice will help you communicate clearly and concisely with your desired audience.

Start with these (you saw them on the previous page):

The data were analyzed using SPSS.

This conclusion was reached by the researchers in the study.

Although manic depression was found in some of the participants, the drug treatment was beneficial for all participants in the study.

Remember, like any other complex skill, practice makes perfect!

A Quick Grammar Summary for APA- 4 Style Writing

It's hard to know how much of a card player you might be, but nowadays you can watch (with relative frequency) competition card games on TV; one of the most popular is Texas No Limit Hold 'em tournaments. If you have watched any of these shows, you have probably heard the announcers say something like "Texas Hold 'em takes a minute to learn, but a lifetime to master." We wish that the rules of English grammar (and APA style and format) took a minute to learn and then a lifetime to master, but alas it is more complicated (in our opinion). If only it took a minute to learn the rules! When we say a lifetime to master, we don't mean that you have to memorize the rules, but you do need to practice the rules and become familiar enough with them so that you can avoid embarrassing mistakes (and some memorization is good for the brain too). There are plenty of tips on how to avoid writing mistakes in this chapter.

Of course, entire textbooks and college courses are devoted to grammar and style. Four of our favorite books include *Woe Is I: The Grammarphobe's Guide to Better English in Plain English* (O'Conner, 1996), *Words Fail Me: What Everyone Who Writes Should Know About Writing* (O'Conner, 1999), *Eats, Shoots & Leaves* (Truss, 2003), and the ever-classic *The Elements of Style* (Strunk & White, 1979). This chapter is just a brief summary of the key components that you need to know about and practice in order to be a better writer of APA style and format. We organize our brief presentation here around parts of a sentence and parts of speech, and we end with common grammatical mistakes that you want to avoid.

Parts of a Sentence

Texas No Limit Hold 'em is a card game with its own set of terminology that must be learned in order to play—terms such as *the flop, the turn, the button, big slick,* and *trips.* If you didn't understand those No Limit Hold 'em terms, you would have a hard time just following the game (much less playing it). The same is true for grammar terminology. If you don't know what is what, then it will be difficult to apply any rules. So we start here with parts of a sentence. By the way, many of these explanations come from Maddox and Scocco (2009), who provide a wonderful resource about basic English grammar available online as a PDF. Next up will be parts of speech, followed by grammatical errors you want to avoid.

Subject: The part of a sentence that is being written about

> The researchers studied the effects of Alzheimer's disease. (The subject is *researchers*.)

Predicate: What we say about the subject of the sentence (the main word in the predicate is the verb).

> I hypothesize that younger adults spend more time on Facebook than older adults. (The predicate is *hypothesize*.)

Phrase: Grammatically related words of a sentence that do not contain the main verb (a sentence fragment that would not exist as a sentence on its own).

> I attended the session at the conference on applying to graduate school. (Both "at the conference" and "on applying to graduate school" are phrases—written alone, they would not stand as sentences.)

Clause: Grammatically related words that do contain a main verb (an independent clause is part of a larger sentence that could stand on its own as a complete sentence). A subordinate clause cannot stand on its own as a sentence because the clause begins with a qualifier, such as *because* or *when*.

> I want to take more statistics, unless the class time conflicts with my work schedule. ("I want to take more statistics" is an independent clause because it can stand on its own as a complete sentence. The second clause, "unless, the class time conflicts with my work schedule," is subordinate, because of the qualifier *unless*).

Object: The part of the sentence that receives the action of the action verb.

> I completed an application to graduate school. (The object of the sentence is *application*, which is the receiver of the action of the verb *completed*.)

Parts of Speech

Next, we provide definitions for each of the parts of speech. This compilation of information comes from multiple sources, including Maddox and Scocco (2009), EzineArticles.com (2009b), and Knight and Ingersoll (1996).

Format Checklist

Words used to describe people, places, things, events, or ideas, nouns are typically the subjects or objects of a sentence. A noun can be singular or plural, which has implications for the verb used with the noun. There are many different types of nouns, but one important distinction for APA format is the proper noun, used to describe a unique person or thing. Proper nouns start with a capital letter (which also applies to APA-format citations).

> Example: "The role of the Rorschach in the clinical intake exam: Impact on psychotherapy effectiveness." In this journal article title from a reference section, Rorschach is capitalized because it is a proper noun, referring to a specific projective test.

Pronoun

A pronoun is a word used to replace a noun, typically used to avoid repetition. There are also singular and plural pronouns, and the pronoun rules differ depending on if the pronoun is used as the subject (e.g., *she, he, they, who*) or the object of the sentence (e.g., *her, him, them, whom*).

> Example: "I hypothesize that students reading online textbook pages will score lower on a multiple-choice test than students reading a traditional textbook." The pronoun *I* takes the place of the author's name.

Adjective

An adjective is a word that describes or qualifies a noun or a pronoun. Adjectives can be found before a noun being described (attributive adjective) or after a verb that follows a noun being described (predicative adjective).

> Example 1: "The **first-year** student signed up for the research study." *First-year* is the attributive adjective describing the student.

> Example 2: "This study is **incomplete**." *Incomplete* is the predicative adjective describing the study.

Article

Articles (*a, and, the*) are actually a special form of adjective called demonstrative adjectives. A definite article (*the*) points out something specific or already introduced. An indefinite article (*a, an*) introduces something unspecific or something mentioned for the first time.

> Example: **The** Method section follows immediately after **the** Introduction section of **a** research paper. *The* in both cases refers to specific parts of a research paper (definite article), and *a* refers to any (unspecific) research paper (indefinite article).

Verb

Verbs typically describe the action within the sentence. Verbs are the most important words in a sentence; they describe the action the subject takes or the subject's state of being.

> Example 1: The student **wrote** a fine paper. *Student* is the subject; *wrote* tells us what the student did.

> Example 2: The student **was happy** with the paper. *Student* is the subject; *was,* with the adjective *happy,* tells us the student's state of being.

There are many different kinds of verbs, and verb forms change depending on, for example, the subject (singular or plural), the tense, the voice (active or passive), and the verb form (regular or irregular).

> Examples: First-person verbs are formed using the subject pronouns **I** and **we**. It is appropriate to write in APA style using first-person pronouns and their accompanying verbs because writing in the first person helps to avoid passive voice (see Chapter 3). Second-person verbs are used with **you**. Third-person verbs are used with the pronouns **he, she, it**, and **they**.

Adverb

Adverbs are words used to modify or qualify a verb, an adjective, another adverb, or clauses.

> Example 1: Participants completed the survey **quickly**. *Quickly* is the adverb that describes how the survey was completed.

> Example 2: Study 1 **successfully** demonstrated the phi phenomenon; **moreover**, Study 1 replicated previous research. Both *successfully* and *moreover* are adverbs; *moreover* is an example of a conjunctive adverb (within a sentence, if a clause begins with a conjunctive adverb, it is preceded by a semicolon).

Preposition

Prepositions are words that combine with nouns or pronouns to provide the connections between two words or clauses. Some prepositions are *about, above, after, among, around, along, at, before, behind, beneath, beside, between, by, down, from, in, into, like, near, of, off, on, out, over, through, to, up, upon, under, until, with,* and *without.*

Examples: My manuscript is **under** review **at** the journal.

Conjunction

Conjunctions are used to join words, phrases, or clauses. There are coordinate conjunctions (*and, but, for, or, nor, so, yet*) and subordinate conjunctions (*that, as, after, before, if, since, when, where, unless*).

Examples: Beth, Eric, **and** Regan enjoyed writing this book. **Because** writing in APA style can be difficult, we thought this book would be helpful to students. *And* is a coordinate conjunction, and *because* is a subordinate conjunction.

Interjection

Interjections are words, phrases, or sentences that express emotion; often, interjections end with an exclamation point or a question mark.

Examples: Take care! Are you kidding me? Interjections are used infrequently in APA-style writing.

Common Grammar Mistakes to Avoid

There are many rules and a lot of advice available to students who want to improve their writing. We certainly applaud you for reading this book and wanting to improve your writing skills. Table 4.1 at the end of the chapter presents some common writing errors to avoid, with brief labels of what the errors are. These are some very common mistakes to avoid that deserve your special attention, and different authors have suggested that if you make any of the grammar mistakes listed next, these types of mistakes make you look "dumb" (Clark, n.d.) or "stupid" (Gilbert, 2006). Those labels may be taking those conclusions a bit far, but you clearly want to avoid making these errors. They make you look like you've written your paper at the last minute and/or suggest you did not have the time or inclination to proofread. Following is a summary of the combined lists (Clark, n.d.; Gilbert, 2006), with examples relevant to APA style and format.

Your—You're

You're is a contraction for the words "you are." Contractions are typically not used in APA-style writing, so this one is easy: *You're* should never appear in your formal research paper. *Your* is a possessive pronoun, and the following example indicates proper use.

Example: We asked participants to answer the open-ended survey question, "What is **your** preferred time of day to study?"

It's—Its

The apostrophe plus *s* ('s) is a typical indicator of a contraction, and as with *you're* above, contractions are not used in formal APA style. When you use *it's*, you mean "it is"; *its* is a possessive pronoun. Notice there is **no** apostrophe in the word *its*, used properly in the following example.

Example: After traversing the open-field exploration box, the experimenter returned the rat to **its** cage for 24 hr rest.

There—Their—They're

First, you should recognize the pattern by now; you won't be using *they're* in APA-style writing because it is a contraction, meaning "they are." Use *there* as a reference to a place ("Put it over there"). *Their* is a plural possessive pronoun, so it needs to refer to more than one object or person and indicate possession.

Example: After the debriefing was complete, **there** were no other tasks for the participants to perform, so the participants were dismissed.

Example: In the driving simulator, I instructed participants to put **their** belongings someplace that would not cause any distractions during the driving tasks.

Loose—Lose

Lose is a verb, meaning to misplace something, whereas *loose* can be an adjective, adverb, or verb depending on usage.

Example: If participants did not arrive to the experiment on time, they would **lose** the opportunity to participate.

Example: In the two-string problem, the knot was too **loose** to allow any other solution.

Example: The teachers let the children **loose** from the classroom for recess.

Example: The man exclaimed, "**Loose** the dog from its crate!"

Affect—Effect

This distinction is a bit tricky, because psychology adds a different twist to the meaning of *affect* and *effect*. Typically, *affect* is used as a verb, such as to act on something; *effect* is used as a noun, such as the bystander effect. But in psychology, *affect* can also be used as a noun to describe an observable feeling or emotion. Although less common, *effect* can be used as a verb to mean accomplishing something or bringing about a result. So all the following are appropriate examples:

Example 1: Prior research **affected** our approach to forming our hypotheses. (*affect* as verb)

Example 2: The newly admitted patient to the hospital ward showed signs of blunt **affect**. (*affect* as noun)

Example 3: The **effect** of the new intervention was moderated by other intervening variables. (*effect* as noun)

Example 4: The researcher was interested in evaluating how the each type of study strategy would **effect** a change in student performance. (*effect* as verb)

i.e.—e.g.

These are two Latin abbreviations that should be used only in a parenthetical phrase (in parentheses) in APA format and that will always be followed by a comma. The Latin abbreviation *i.e.* stands for *id est* in Latin, meaning "that is." The Latin abbreviation *e.g.* stands for *exempli gratia,* meaning "for example" or "such as."

Example 1: The appropriate analyses were completed post hoc (**i.e.**, after the fact).

Example 2: Survey responses to the career-path question were coded based on eventual outcome (**e.g.**, bachelor's degree leading to a good job, bachelor's degree leading to a graduate school application).

Lay—Lie

Mentioned already in Chapter 3, *lay* is a verb that means "to place" or "put down," such as placing an object on the table. *Lie* can be used as a verb, as in "taking a horizontal position" or lying down, or *lie* can be used as a noun, as in "I told a lie."

Example 1: After the students recorded their reaction times, we asked students to **lay** the stopwatches on their desk.

Example 2: The key to lowering one's heart rate is to recline and **lie** still while practicing the indicated breathing exercises.

Then—Than

Then can be used as an adverb, adjective, or noun, which often applies to a description of time. *Than* can be used as a conjunction or preposition. Typically, *than* is used as part of a comparison.

Example 1: After the experiment was completed, participants **then** were allowed to ask questions during the debriefing.

Example 2: It took longer to complete Study 1 **than** it did to complete Study 2.

That—Which

Although the rules are actually more complicated than the summary provided here, typically, *that* is used as a restrictive clause; a restrictive clause introduces essential information. Also, in the typical sentence form, the word *that* is not preceded by a comma. *Which* is typically used as a nonrestrictive clause; a nonrestrictive clause introduces extra information. A comma precedes *which* in this instance (Gaertner-Johnston, 2006).

Example 1: A well-written literature review is one **that** summarizes and organizes the diverse research on a topic of interest.

Example 2: Students sometimes struggle with knowing what level of detail to write about in the Introduction section, **which** is to say that not all students struggle with this task.

Could of, Would of—Could have, Would have

According to Blue (2000), there is no such phrase as "could of" in English. What happens is that when we are speaking, many times we do not articulate well, so when we say "could have" it actually sounds like "could of." In fact, if you were to use the contraction form, "could've" sounds very similar to pronouncing "could of." However, the proper phrases are *could have, would have, must have,* and so on; our writing should reflect the proper usage.

Example 1: I **could have** used a between-groups or within-groups design.

Example 2: If I had known, I **would have** attended that conference last spring.

Avoid these 10 common errors, and you will show your audience (your professors) that you are conscientious about your writing and that you pay attention to details. For more types of errors (with examples), see Table 4.1. We've bolded the changes in the correct sentences so you can find exactly what was changed.

As you continue to practice your writing ability, these rules should eventually become second nature. Although it may be handy to know the name of the rule and what parts of speech are involved, we believe it is much more important to infuse these rules into your writing to avoid making the mistakes. You may not know that the first draft of a sentence you have just written in a research paper includes a dangling participle or a misplaced modifier, but we want you to practice enough so that you can "hear" or "see" the error and correct it while revising your draft. Writing is a "use it or lose it" skill. Practicing your writing with helpful feedback is essential if you want to be able to think and write clearly.

Rest assured, to this day we write and rewrite our papers. We go back and check our work before we pass it on. We try to get another set of eyes to proofread for grammatical errors (or hire good editors). Very few folks have the magical gift of grammatical writing come naturally.

Table 4.1 Common Writing Errors to Avoid

Common Grammatical Errors	Example of the Error	Error Corrected
1. No comma after an introductory element	Well it wasn't really true.	Well**,** it wasn't really true.
2. Vague pronoun reference	John told his father that his car had been stolen.	John told his father that his **father's** car had been stolen.
3. No comma in compound sentence	I like to eat but I hate to gain weight.	I like to eat**,** but I hate to gain weight.
4. Wrong word	His F in math enhanced his alarm about his D in chemistry.	His F in math **amplified** his alarm about his D in chemistry.
5. Missing comma(s) with a nonrestrictive element	The students who had unsuccessfully concealed their participation in the prank were expelled.	The students**,** who had unsuccessfully concealed their participation in the prank**,** were expelled.
6. Wrong or missing verb ending	I often use to go to town.	I often **used** to go to town.
7. Wrong or missing preposition	Cottonwood Grille is located at Boise.	Cottonwood Grille is located **in** Boise.
8. Comma splice	Chloe liked the cat, however, she was allergic to it.	Chloe liked the cat**;** however, she was allergic to it.
9. Missing or misplaced possessive apostrophe	Student's backpacks weigh far too much.	Student**s'** backpacks weigh far too much.
10. Unnecessary shift in tense	I was happily watching TV when suddenly my sister attacks me.	I was happily watching TV when suddenly my sister **attacked** me.
11. Unnecessary shift in pronoun	When one is tired, you should sleep.	When **you** are tired, you should sleep.

Common Grammatical Errors	Example of the Error	Error Corrected
12. Sentence fragment (second part)	He went shopping in the local sports store. An outing he usually enjoyed.	He went shopping in the local sports store, **an** outing he usually enjoyed.
13. Wrong tense or verb form	I would not have said that if I thought it would have shocked her.	I would not have said that if I thought it would **shock** her.
14. Lack of subject-verb agreement	Having many close friends, especially if you've known them for a long time, are a great help in times of trouble.	Having many close friends, especially if you've known them for a long time, **is** a great help in times of trouble.
15. Missing comma in a series	Students eat, sleep and do homework.	Students eat, sleep**,** and do homework.
16. Lack of agreement between pronoun and antecedent	When someone plagiarizes from material on a website, they are likely to be caught.	When **you** plagiarize from material on a website, **you** are likely to be caught.
17. Unnecessary comma(s) with a restrictive element	The novel, that my teacher assigned, was very boring.	The novel that my teacher assigned was very boring.
18. Run-on or fused sentence	He loved the seminar he even loved the readings.	He loved the seminar**;** he even loved the readings.
19. Dangling or misplaced modifier	After being put to sleep, a small incision is made below the navel.	A small incision is made below the navel **after the patient is anesthetized**.
20. Its/it's confusion	Its a splendid day for everyone.	**It's** a splendid day for everyone.

Note. The examples in the table are adapted from Gottschalk and Hjortshoj (2004) and Landrum (2008).

Thou Shalt Not Steal (or Be Lazy) 5

Plagiarism and How to Avoid It

Someone once said every good idea worth thinking has already been thought. Or at least it went something like that. If there is even a hint of truth to this statement, it is clear that whenever we write a paper, we are probably writing something that someone has said before or thought about before. Now if we just left it at that and moved on—note there is no citation in the first sentence—it would be plagiarism. If we were not trying to make a point, we would have ended the first sentence with a citation in parenthesis (e.g., Lorde, 1984). More on this paraphrase in a moment. When assigned to explicitly do a review of research on a certain topic or when writing the introduction to a research paper, a large part of which is a literature review, you have to refer to other published work. If you use someone's ideas, you have to give them credit. If you do not, you are plagiarizing their work and committing intellectual theft. Plagiarizing is wrong, unethical, and just plain not a good idea. Worse, plagiarism can result in a failing grade or sometimes even more severe consequences such as getting expelled from school.

But I Didn't Know . . .

First the tough love: Not knowing how to correctly cite your information, or that you had to, is not an acceptable excuse. It's the same thing as telling a police officer that you didn't know the speed limit was only 55 mph. Ignorance doesn't work in that case, and it won't work when it comes to not appropriately citing the information you use in your papers. If you use information or data from someone else's work, you have to cite it (or else it is stealing). Not being able to locate the source of your information, and so not citing it, is not an acceptable excuse for not citing your source either (it is being lazy). Not knowing that someone else had the same idea or thought is somewhat more understandable. Sometimes we read something and forget we did. Then we remember the gist of what we once read but forget we read it somewhere, thinking instead that it is our own wonderful idea. If you ever feel like you are using information from somewhere else, take the trouble to find it. It may not be too difficult. In fact, the source of the statement paraphrased in the first sentence eluded us until a Google search (0.13 secs) and a little digging (0.45 secs) suggested that Audre Lorde is the source. Lorde (1984) said, "There are no new ideas. There are only new ways of making them felt" (p. 39). The Bible provides a similar sentiment: "What has been will be again, what has been done will be done again; there is nothing new under the sun" (Ecclesiastes 1:9, New International Version). What is the long and short of the story? Make sure you cite your sources. In this chapter, we spell out some of the key ways to avoid being a plagiarizer.

It Sounds Like a Bad Word

Plagiarism really is despicable. Although what we said in the opening paragraph seems simple, this is exactly what plagiarism is: using someone else's ideas without giving them credit. Many students do not realize how dishonest this act really is. Even more disturbing, many students know it is wrong and still try to pull it off. Yes, we know the draw of writing an "A" paper is appealing, and using someone else's A paper may seem like an easy way to get an A on your paper, but it is really no laughing matter. Remember, it is also getting exceedingly easy for faculty to track down plagiarism. Sometimes we notice suspicious-looking sentences—say, sentences that seem overly technical or different from the bulk of a student paper—and just put the sentence into a search engine (either a specialized search engine, like turnitin.com, or even into google.com). This simple move has resulted in the location of online sources of the sentence (often within the first few search results) that have not been cited properly—or at all. Many universities subscribe to sites that will check whether papers have been plagiarized. So again, it may be easy to plagiarize, but it is also getting easier to track it. Make sure you do not forget to cite the sources of the information you use in your papers. In fact, the ways to avoid plagiarizing are pretty easy. Cite your sources, use quotations if need be, and even better, paraphrase (and cite). Each of these ways is somewhat easy to master as you shall soon see. The best way to avoid this problem is to write down the source information, but put aside the actual source you are using when you are writing. That way, you have to write in your own words. Putting away the original book or article will help you avoid the mistake of writing something directly from the source and forgetting to include the citation. It will avoid the common problem of just reorganizing the same words or deleting a few words and assuming that the thoughts are now yours and not those of the original author.

Quoting: More Than Just a Copy and Paste

It is easy to want to play it completely safe and directly quote—that is, copy exactly what is written in the original source. You then cite the source in the text (see guides for this in Chapter 7), using the correct punctuation, and you are home free. Or so it seems. First, let's look at how you would do this seemingly simple task in APA format, and then we'll talk a little more about why you should limit your quotations.

When you are quoting, you need to have handy the author, year, and page number or numbers for in-text citations. If your source is a website, you will need the paragraph number. Now comes the fine-tuning. Short quotations (up to 40 words) can be cordoned off with double quotation marks (" ") but can be within the text. Here's an example:

> Some psychologists have used colorful phrases to describe how the mind works, such as its being "as one great blooming, buzzing confusion" (James, 1890/1950, p. 462).

Note that the second set of double quotation marks is followed by the standard in-text citation (author, year) but also includes the page number. Also notice in the example that there is not a period at the end of the sentence that is quoted. The period comes after the citation is completed. If the quotation comes from a single page, use a single *p* followed by a period and a space before the page number; if the quotation spans two pages, use a double *p* followed by a period, a space, and the range of pages (e.g., pp. 144–145). For online sources without page numbers, use the abbreviation "para." for paragraph instead of "p." for pages, or you can use the paragraph symbol (¶). You will need to count down to the paragraph on the website that you took the quotation from and use that to indicate where the original text can be found (e.g., para. 7). Sometimes the quotation may be within the sentence and not at the end as shown in the preceding example. The sentence will now look like this:

> William James (1890/1950) provides us with colorful phrases to describe how the mind works, such as its being "as one great blooming, buzzing confusion" (p. 462) and wrote at length about how consciousness may work.

If you really need to directly quote more than 40 words (not something you should aim to do), you do not need the double quotation marks. Instead, you give the quotation its own place of honor in your paper by starting it on a new line and indenting the block of text making up the quotation by half an inch from the left margin; the right margin, however, is not indented (APA, 2010a). Your citation now comes at the end of the block. This time, the parenthesis in which the text is cited follows the period at the end of the block quotation. There is no additional period after the parenthesis, and the entire quotation is double-spaced (like the rest of your paper). It looks like this:

> It is difficult to examine how students study. Some of the problems inherent in such research are demonstrated by the results of a recent study on the topic.
>
> > Studying with a friend was negatively correlated to exam scores in our study. Perhaps students need to be trained in the best way to study with a friend. Instructors can model how students should make up examples with the material and quiz each other. For some students "studying with a friend" may mean sitting on a couch reading notes and chatting with the television on. Whereas you can control and monitor what a student is doing in a laboratory experiment on studying, a simple questionnaire measure may not accurately tap into what students do as they study in college. (Gurung, Weidert, & Jeske, 2010, p. 33)

One of the reasons we caution against the use of long quotations is that for publications (journal articles or books), one often needs written permission from the author of the source material or, more accurately, from the owner of the copyright for the work. Obtaining permission can be expensive and time-consuming. Now to be fair, the long arm of the copyright police is probably not going to track down a student paper and fine you for not paying for the quotation or asking permission, but the time and expense involved in obtaining permission are still good reasons not to use long quotations. Another reason is that you do not want your paper to be a string of someone else's words. Including someone else's words within your text usually creates a choppy flow to your writing, because your style of writing is usually different from that of the other authors you quote. Sometimes students think that if they string together a sequence of direct quotations, writing the paper is simplified because less of the paper actually needs to be written. Avoid this strategy; stringing together a bunch of direct quotations is not scholarly writing.

There are some instances when a direct word-for-word quotation is critical. When you are using a previously published scale or questionnaire, you should use the exact wording of the original. Particularly colorful or well-worded sentences or ideas are also often better directly quoted. One of the founders of American psychology, William James, was a particularly colorful writer. His pre-20th-century English and word choices make for fun reading (and the psychology is pretty good too), as shown in the earlier example. Sometimes an idea may be exceedingly complex or composed of unique or newly generated terms or phrases, which is another good reason to quote directly. In all cases, be sure you have a clear understanding of the quotation so that it fits well within the paragraph in which you include it. These exceptions notwithstanding, it is preferable to convey the gist of the idea or thoughts by paraphrasing.

Paraphrasing: In Your Own Words

When you paraphrase, you are essentially discussing someone else's ideas or results in your own words. You still have to cite your source, but given you are not copying (right?) the other material word for word, you do not need to use double quotation marks around the sentence. You do not need to cite the page or paragraph number (in text) either, *but* it is a good idea to do so (APA, 2010a). One of our friends provided a useful tip on how to paraphrase. Our friend (remembering what a teacher told him) said that paraphrasing is something like reading a journal article, thinking about it, and then turning to your neighbor and describing the main gist of what was read in your own words (W. Fulton, personal communication, June 24, 1995). Yes, we paraphrased that. As we mentioned earlier, the easiest way to paraphrase and avoid using the original author's words is to close the book (or the site you have opened) and not have the original source in front of you when you are attempting to get across the main points. But keep this in mind: This technique will help you determine if you really understand the main gist. If you have trouble putting it in your own words, you might need to reread the original source for a better understanding.

That's Really Sic [and Not a Typo]

Sometimes you may want or need to directly quote someone or some text that contains misspellings, poor grammar, or poor punctuation. How do you do it without making it look like you could not copy correctly or perhaps you made a mistake? Easy. Latin to the rescue! You insert the word [*sic*] in italics and brackets, right in the quotation where the troublesome language resides. *Sic* means "thus" or "so" and implies the word was "intentionally so written" ("Sic," 2003, p. 1156). The brackets show that the word is not part of the quotation.

An Author's License (Yours): Modifying Source Material

For the most part when you paraphrase, you are modifying the words used in the original material, but you are not modifying the actual message, idea, or finding. But there are times when you use a direct quotation, and you want to make minor changes to what you are using. For example, sometimes you may not want to use an entire sentence. Some authors can write very long sentences, and the key element may be in the first part. This is where you can use three spaced periods, called an ellipsis (. . .). Interestingly, if the omitted information is at the end of the sentence, then you place the ellipses after the period before continuing with the rest of the quotation. If the omitted information comes at the end of the quotation, there's no need for an ellipsis. Likewise, if the omitted information comes before the text you want to quote, there's no need for an ellipsis.

There is one other modification to consider, although you should probably not use it too much. It looks like a handy tool and it is, but it can also be easily overused. If you want to stress a word or phrase in a quotation, italicize the word or phrase and then follow it with the phrase [emphasis added] using brackets and not parentheses.

> Intuitively useful study strategies may not be as useful as they may seem. Gurung, Weidert, and Jeske (2010) found that "some often recommended strategies turned out to correlate *negatively* [emphasis added] with exam scores" (p. 32).

But I Can Freely Use My Own Work, Right?

So you have written a great paper on the history of the Roman Empire for one class. Now you need to write a shorter paper on how Roman society went into decline. You already tackled this topic in your big Roman paper. Should you just cut the relevant section of your big paper and turn it in as your short paper? Believe it or not there is something known as *self-plagiarism*. Self-plagiarism explicitly refers to work that has already been published. "The new document must constitute an original contribution to knowledge, and only the amount of previously published material necessary to understand that contribution should be included" (APA, 2010a, p. 16). In other words don't present previous work as if it is brand new. Does this apply to you presenting what you wrote for one class to an instructor of another class? Honestly, this is a judgment call for you to make. The best solution is to check with your instructor to see if your modification of another paper would be acceptable.

How About This for a Plagiarism Awareness Exercise?

As we write this guide about APA style, we are of course providing the details of the information from the APA *PM* by covering the many rules of writing in APA style without plagiarizing. This in itself is an exercise in using appropriate citations and paraphrasing. Want models of how to avoid plagiarism? You can map chapters of our book against the corresponding material in the APA *PM* (APA, 2010a). Just for the (somewhat geeky) fun of it, place this *EasyGuide* and the *PM* side by side and open up to a similar topic. Given that we have paid exquisite attention to ensuring our material is adequately cited while giving you the most accurate information about APA style and format, you are in the good position of being able to see a book-length example about how one (or three in our case) can write explicitly about a clear source without committing the sin of plagiarism. Enjoy.

Avoiding Biased Language 6

Psychologists are interested in the behavior of individuals, either as a means of forming generalizations about human behavior (called a *nomothetic* approach) or for the sake of understanding the unique behavior of one person (called an *idiographic* approach). This focus on the individual, regardless of the research approach taken, necessitates both common sense and sensibility to the uniqueness of individuals. When we are not careful, we take mental shortcuts that allow us to describe a group of individuals quickly, but that description could be far from accurate (which can lead to prejudice, discrimination, and stereotyping). APA guidelines are clear about the preference for accuracy in description even if sentence structures become more complicated and an economy of words is lost (APA, 2010a). When describing humans involved in psychological research, it is better to be accurate and complete than to be overly concise and vague. Taking mental shortcuts with our descriptions of research participants can lead to biased language and misunderstandings about both the participants and the intent of the research.

The Fundamental Lesson: View People as Individuals First

One of the basic lessons that physicians learn in medical school is "first, do no harm." With regard to the potential for biased language when describing human participants in psychology, the fundamental lesson is "view people as individuals first." That is, individuals are much more than the label attached to them by others. Describing the complexity of a unique human being with a singular label is at best a mental shortcut and lazy and at worst demeaning, prejudicial and biased and to say the least could be harmful. With a nod to Gestalt psychology, people are more than the sum of their labels. Avoiding labels applies to all participants in research, not just participants from a clinical setting. So the preference would be to refer to someone as "a person with schizophrenia" rather than a "schizophrenic" (literally, putting the person first in the phrase). Rather than describing the correlation between GPA and high self-esteem students, it would be better to report the correlation between GPA and students who report high self-esteem levels. Ulrich (2005) shared the example that it is preferable to describe "people with diabetes" rather than "diabetics." Diabetics have a universe of behaviors that is much more complex than the singular description of diabetes. Not all diabetics share the same characteristics at one time over the course of the disorder; therefore, it is actually more accurate to state "people with diabetes" because that connotes different individuals who happen to share one characteristic, but in many cases that may be their only common characteristic.

Specific Recommendations for Reducing Bias: Nonsexist Language and Other Areas

It is important to provide concrete examples of possible bias, because we may not even be aware of this bias during our writing. There are typically no "absolutes," but we do make specific suggestions about what to avoid ("biased") and the preferred approach ("unbiased"). Of course, *preferred* could be seen in the eye of the beholder, but we base these recommendations not only on our teaching experience but also on various sources (APA, 2010a, 2010b; Driscoll, 2009b; Kessler & McDonald, 2008). Because gender bias in writing remains a difficult problem to solve, we address this topic separately at the close of this chapter.

Sexual Orientation

Perhaps there is no other characteristic so essential to each of us yet at times so complicated to describe as our sexual orientation. Writing in APA style necessitates accuracy and precision, but at the same time sensitivity to individual difference and honoring the preferences for the naming of groups of individuals who may be dramatically different, yet share similar sexual orientation characteristics. Specificity is preferred. For instance, the broad term *homosexuality* is too vague; even using the singular term *gay* is not precise. The preferred terminology to use is *lesbian, gay man, bisexual man,* and *bisexual woman* (APA, 2010a). This level of precision helps prevent misunderstandings about the precise nature of the individuals in a study.

It is also important to not mix descriptions of sexual orientation with presumptions about sexual behavior. Once again, specificity is key. In a Results section, for example, rather than writing, "Forty-two percent of gays reported at least one instance of homosexual fantasies," it would be better to add more precision; "Forty-two percent of gay men reported at least one instance of male-male sexual fantasies." The first sentence is much too vague to convey the accurate information needed in a Results section. Descriptions of sexual behavior should be precise as well. So instead of asking the survey question "At what age did you first have sexual intercourse," it would be better to reword that question as (a) "At what age did you first have penile-vaginal intercourse" or (b) "At what age did you first have sexual intercourse or sex with another person?" Although the sentence structure is more complex, the information gleaned from the survey responses should be better because participants will understand precisely what you mean (with dual benefits—avoiding bias and improving clarity).

Racial and Ethnic Identity

As a general rule, the more precision that you can use to describe the participants of your research, the better; this added precision comes with an important bonus—a reduced likelihood of using terms with racial or ethnic bias. First, let's address the difference in those two terms—race versus ethnicity. Of course people's definitions of these topics can differ, but here goes. Ethnicity tends to refer to groups of people who self-identify with each other, typically on the basis of common ancestry. Examples of ethnic groups in America would include American Indians, African Americans, Latinos, and Chinese; but you also might include Irish Americans and German Americans here too. Race tends to refer to a biological variety of species with similar anatomical traits; the term may also be used by some external entity to divide or categorize people based on certain physical characteristics (O'Neil, 2006).

For example, the U.S. Census Bureau asks separate questions about race and ethnicity. When asking about race, the Census Bureau uses the following categories:

- White
- Black or African American
- American Indian or Alaska Native
- Asian
- Native Hawaiian and Other Pacific Islander

In the census format, a person can also select more than one of these categories, and there are write-in areas as well. Ethnicity is captured by just two categories in census questions:

- Hispanic or Latino
- Not Hispanic or Latino

The idea underlying this sequence of questions about race and ethnicity in this case is that a person of Hispanic or Latino heritage can be of any race; that is, race and ethnicity are treated as different concepts (U.S. Census Bureau, 2008).

These ideas are important for our communication of race and ethnic data when writing in APA style, but our preference is to be even more precise than Census Bureau categories when possible. So when referring to American Indians, naming specific tribes involved would be preferable, or in some situations using the First Nations designation. Avoid the use of the term *minority*, because without additional context, it is difficult to determine the minority of what. Similarly, rather than a White versus non-White distinction, specify the individual subgroups that compose the non-White participants in a study (African Americans, American Indians, or Alaskan Natives). Even when using proper terminology, such as Hispanic or Latino, if you have more detailed information about the nations or regions of the participants, be more specific—Cuban, Guatemalan, Salvadoran, and so on (APA, 2010a). In fact, you can be more specific than Mexican Americans. For example, Mexican Americans in Texas often prefer the term *Tejano*.

Disabilities

Following the advice of this chapter's opening mantra—put people first—will serve you well when discussing individuals with disabilities (notice the wording in this sentence: "individuals with disabilities," not "disabled people"). The disability a person possesses does not completely define that person; it is but one aspect of someone's situation or behavior (i.e., a person's physical health or mental health). So rather than discuss an ADHD child, it would be better to discuss a child with ADHD or a child who exhibits ADHD symptoms. It is preferable to be more precise in describing the potential disabilities rather than applying a large categorical label that masks the complexities and individual differences of the persons with a particular disorder or condition. Rather than saying "schizophrenics were divided into the treatment and control groups," it would be better to describe the individuals with schizophrenia in greater detail: "those individuals with paranoid schizophrenic symptoms" or "those individuals with catatonic schizophrenic symptoms," and so on.

One last note about writing about disabilities: Avoid emotionally charged words or words that are inaccurate in describing the totality of a person. So avoid using words such as *crippled, handicapped, retarded, physically challenged,* and *stroke victim*; these descriptors are often inaccurate and offensive to people with a particular disability. Being sensitive to these perceptions will help you avoid using biased language in your writing.

Occupations

Related to issues of gender bias, a number of occupations over time used the embedded *man* as part of the description of the career or occupation. In Table 6.1, we present a listing of original or biased terms and then substitute unbiased terms for use. In some cases, you will have to rewrite the structure of the sentence to make the sentence grammatically correct. This is a small price to pay to avoid gender bias as it relates to occupations.

Table 6.1 Biased Versus Unbiased Occupational Titles

Biased Occupational Title	Unbiased Occupational Title
Businessman, businesswoman	Businessperson, business executive, entrepreneur
Chairman	Chair, chairperson, head, presiding officer
Congressman	Senator, representative
Fireman	Firefighter
Foreman	Supervisor
Mailman	Mail carrier
Male nurse	Nurse
Newsman	Reporter
Policeman, policewoman	Police officer
Salesman	Sales clerk, sales representative
Spokesman	Representative, leader, spokesperson
Steward, stewardess	Flight attendant
Woman doctor	Doctor

Gender and Pronouns: With an Indefinite Recommendation

The generic *he* is well-embedded in our writing (Kessler & McDonald, 2008), and when writing scientifically with precision, we must work to avoid this assumption. This is no easy task, because the presumption is pervasive in our culture. Not only did you see the occupational examples in Table 6.1, but see Table 6.2 for more examples of the lack of inclusivity we often exhibit in our writing (Driscoll, 2009b; Kessler & McDonald, 2008).

APA style strongly recommends that you avoid the use of *he* or *she* whenever possible. Avoiding such gendered pronouns helps to minimize confusion on the reader's part. However, this does not mean that the awkward phrase "he/she" should be substituted. It is a better alternative to rewrite the sentence so that the gendered pronoun is avoided altogether. Wagner et al. (2009) made some specific recommendations on how to do that and conform to APA style. See the following examples for rewriting suggestions to avoid biased language:

Table 6.2 Gender References: Less Versus More Inclusive Terms

Less Inclusive	More Inclusive
Man, men	Person, people
Mankind	People, humanity, human beings
Founding fathers	Founders, forebears
Gentlemen's agreement	Informal agreement
Manpower	Workforce
Man (as a verb, to man)	Staff, operate
Man's achievements	Human achievements
Man-made	Synthetic, manufactured, machine made
Common man	Average person, ordinary person
Man-hours	Staff hours

- Rephrase the sentence to avoid the necessity of using *he* or *she*.

  Biased: After the study, he determined that the main effect of age was statistically significant.

  Unbiased: The author found age to be statistically significant at the conclusion of the study.

- Use a plural noun or plural pronoun, meaning that you can then use *they* or *their*, but try to do this sparingly.

  Biased: Men and women were tested individually; either he or she flipped a coin to see who would go first.

  Unbiased: Men and women were tested individually; they flipped a coin to see who would go first.

- When possible, replace the pronoun with an article; instead of *her* or *him*, use *the*.

  Biased: The confederate then asked her research participant to complete the survey.

  Unbiased: The confederate then asked the research participant to complete the survey.

- Drop the pronoun, and see if the sentence still makes sense; often it will.

  Biased: The experimenter checked to see if his class points were recorded.

  Unbiased: The experimenter checked to see if class points were recorded.

- Replace the pronoun with a noun such as *person, individual, researcher,* or *participant.*

  Biased: We wanted to determine if his or her prior experiences influenced current attitudes.

  Unbiased: We wanted to determine if the person's prior experiences influenced current attitudes.

One other method of avoiding gender bias in your scientific writing is to use indefinite pronouns rather than gendered pronouns (Driscoll, 2009a). Use indefinite pronouns such as *everybody, everyone, anybody,* and *anyone* to avoid gender bias. Check out the following examples.

Biased: Anyone wanting to sign up for the experiment needs to use his or her student identification number.

Unbiased: One wanting to sign up for the experiment needs to use one's student identification number.

Or just rewrite the sentence to avoid the gender reference altogether.

Biased: Anyone wanting to sign up for the experiment needs to use his or her student identification number.

Unbiased: Student identification numbers are necessary for signing up for the experiment.

As it turns out, even with all the available resources to help us avoid gender bias, we still tend to be sexist in our writing. A study published in the *British Journal of Social Psychology* (Hegarty et al., 2010) reported research showing that some of the 16th-century naming conventions still strongly exist today. For example, we say "Mr. and Mrs." and not the reverse—"his and hers towels," but typically not "hers and his towels." If you really think about it, why should the "Mr." be said (and written) first; why not list "Mrs." first? When we think about the names of heterosexual couples (especially individuals we do not know), the researchers reported, we tend to say the man's name before the woman's—David and Sarah, Brad and Angelina, Romeo and Juliet—rather than the other way around. The one exception that the researchers noted was when we know the couple and we know one person better than the other. So if you are sending a holiday card to your sister and her husband, you are more likely to address it to your sister first (Janet and Dan) rather than reverse order. We still need to be vigilant about possible occurrences of gender bias.

With attention to detail, with practice, and by following the advice provided in this chapter, you can improve the accuracy and precision of your scientific writing as well as avoid bias and be respectful of the individual differences (on so many different levels—gender, sexual orientation, race, ethnicity, disabilities, occupation) that make humans so unique and fascinating to study.

SECTION III

Writing With (APA) Style

Getting Down to Business

Whodunnit (or Said It)? 7

Citing References in Text

When it comes to citing works you have read—essentially, giving credit to the authors of information you are using in your paper—there is good news and bad news. The good news is that doing it right is not too difficult at all with even a little practice. The bad news is that it is one of the most common things for students to get wrong when first learning to write in APA style. It is also one of *the* easiest mistakes for your instructor to pick up on. One quick look at your paper, even with eyes squinted partially shut, and one can tell if you have cited your sources correctly. This of course assumes you have cited your sources in the first place. Not mentioning where you got your information, ideas, or findings is called plagiarism, an even bigger problem that we discussed in the previous chapter. The bottom line is that science involves building on past findings, and even a paper breaking new ground has to connect new ideas to related information from the past. This information has to be properly referenced and cited, which is what this chapter is all about.

A Good Rule of Thumb

If you are writing something that is not 100% your own original idea, whether your opinion, your observations, or your findings from a study you conducted, you should cite your source. A citation can range from a statistic you use to start your paper (e.g., "There are more bars than grocery stores in the state of Wisconsin") to a result or conclusion of a research study that is pertinent to your paper (e.g., "Underage drinking is associated with cognitive processing impairments"). In both cases, you need to cite your source in the main part of your paper (any part up to the reference section) using an in-text citation. You then write out the complete information on the source of the data in APA style in the aptly named References section. We describe the basics of the References section in Chapter 10.

Ready, Cite, GO

So let's set the stage for citing. You are writing a paper for class. After you received the assignment and figured out your topic, you conducted a search for what is written on the topic. You used online databases through your school library website or a similar source and generated a number of journal articles, book chapters, and books that you want to read for information to possibly include in your paper. You now must use the online databases to get either the full text or complete articles. You can save PDF files to your computer (go green) or you can print them out. You might be interested in going beyond the electronic resources and checking out a book, or perhaps you need to copy a journal article not available in full text online, in which case you will be heading to the library. Regardless of how you do it, the key is to have the complete article(s) in front of you (including all of the references in the article you are retrieving). Now you can read them and see if you want to use them in your paper. If you want to use them, then you are ready to cite them in the text.

An important side note: Your initial searches (perhaps you used Google or another online search engine) may have dug up some online webpages with information (e.g., Wikipedia). A word of advice: Don't use or cite Wikipedia or personal webpages in your paper (even if they are personal pages of famous researchers). Wikipedia can be a great place to get ideas, but it should not be the last place you look, and it is a lousy source to cite in a formal research paper. By this, we mean the best sources of information for your papers are peer-reviewed publications, whether they are journal articles or book chapters or books. Note we are not saying you should use the information from Wikipedia without citing it so no one knows where you got it; that would be plagiarism (see Chapter 5). There are many useful credible websites you may use as well. For example, more and more government information (e.g., National Institute of Mental Health) is available on the web. The difference is that we can't change what is posted on the National Institute of Mental Health website, but we can change what is posted on Wikipedia, which alerts us to a potential concern about credibility of that source.

Want the most impressive type of source of information? A journal article is the best source of information according to many academics. In the nonacademic world, *journal* may conjure up images of something in which you jot down daily reflections. That's not what we mean. We do not mean *magazine* either. Here we mean "scholarly publications" of either write-ups of research or theoretical discussions. Most areas of psychology have journals dedicated to publishing research from their respective areas (e.g., *Journal of Experimental Psychology, Journal of Abnormal Psychology*). Mind you, not all journals have the word *Journal* in the title (e.g., *Developmental Psychology, Psychology and Aging*). Researchers write journal articles that are then edited and reviewed by the authors' peers (i.e., "peer reviewed") and in many cases have to follow stringent criteria. Although magazines sometimes feature contributions by researchers, more often than not, for magazine articles there is no peer review of the work written by paid journalists. Such sources include *Psychology Today* (hint: not a good citation for a research paper)—although *Psychology Today* might be good for ideas about a research paper. Most books are reviewed before publication, but the process of review is very different (e.g., publishers hire experts to review the manuscript before publication). Conclusions and data from a journal article carry more weight.

In-Text Citation Basics

Once you want to cite an article and you have it ready (online or on paper next to you), there is important information to look for. There are two main parts to an in-text citation, the author and the date of publication (note how this differs from an MLA citation; in MLA, you would cite the author, then the page number from which the information came). In the majority of cases, the author will be an individual or individuals. In some cases, the source will be an organization or its website (e.g., American Psychological Association, 2010). When your source is not an organization, use only the author's or authors' last name(s), a comma, and the year of publication (e.g., Gurung & Schwartz, 2009). Notice we *did not* include any information about the authors' first names. One common error students make when first learning APA style is including an author's first name or initial(s). A basic citation of one author will look like this:

> Starting studying early and reading material prior to and after class were not related to exam scores (Gurung, 2005).

If there are two authors, separate the two authors by the ampersand symbol, "&." A basic citation of two authors will look like this:

> There are a variety of ways to measure how students study and which methods work better than others (Gurung & Schwartz, 2009).

When you want to cite articles written by three or more authors (up to five), separate the last two authors by the ampersand symbol (&), and separate the preceding ones with a comma or commas. Make a note to yourself that you even need to include a comma after the second-to-last author, before the ampersand symbol. Not adding this comma is another common error students typically make. The basic citation of three to five authors looks like this:

> A truly fun and readable book on APA style can successfully do away with excessive and unneeded jargon (Schwartz, Landrum, & Gurung, 2012).

Multiple-Author Bonus

Every time you cite the work of one or two authors, you have to cite the author or authors every time, which for two authors means including both last names each time you cite the work. However, if you cite the work of three or more authors (up to five) more than once, you cite all the names only the first time (as illustrated in the previous example). The next time you cite the source, you use only the first author's last name and then the Latin abbreviation "et al.," which means "and others" (note no period after "et" but a period after "al"); then another comma; and finally the publication year. You leave out all the other authors' last names. So let's say you want to cite this APA style guide more than once; the second and all other citations would look something like this:

> This is your sentence that refers again to that great APA style guide (Schwartz et al., 2012).

When you are thinking about these sentences grammatically, remember that et al. stands for "and others" and that your verb needs to agree with a plural noun (*others*).

If the source you are citing has more than five authors, you only have to cite the last name of the first author followed by the Latin abbreviation et al. (again with a period after "al"), even the first time you cite that work. Although this seems like a raw deal for the other authors, whose names do not see the light of day in any in-text citations, their names **are** included in the Reference section. So whether the first, second, or ninth time you cite the article, you use only the first author's last name in the body of your paper. If you cite a source with more than seven authors, the rules are the same in the text of your paper, but the rules change in the Reference section. In the case of more than seven authors, in your Reference section you include the names (last names, first name initials) for the first six authors followed by three ellipsis points, and end with an ampersand (&) followed by the last author's name. The names of coauthors who are seventh, eighth, and ninth will not see their names included in either your text or your Reference section. Now that is truly a raw deal!

A Variation on the Theme

The examples of in-text citations shown earlier illustrate the preferred way to write out information with citations within parentheses. You will note that in all cases, the authors are placed at the end of the sentence. Sometimes you may want to cite the author(s) within the flow of your sentence. In such cases, the biggest difference is that you use the word *and* where you would use an ampersand (&) in all the previous examples. Use the ampersand symbol only in parentheses. You still need the publication date in parentheses at the end of the citation:

Schwartz, Landrum, and Gurung (2012) have certainly written one of the most readable books about APA style ever created in the history of humankind.

Some Curve Balls

We have sketched out the most common in-text citations you will need. The previous examples will probably account for over 85% of your citation needs. That said, here are some interesting citation conundrums you might come across, and we certainly don't want to leave you hanging. We list the issue and then the solution.

What Do I Do When I Need to Cite More Than One Article in the Same Spot?

Sometimes you need more than one citation to make a point. In such cases, there are two major rules to follow. First, you separate the sources by a semicolon (;); then you put the articles in **alphabetical order using the first author's last name** as the main reference point (even if that makes the years published out of chronological order). You then list all the different articles. For example:

> When objectified, a woman's body, or parts of her body, are separated from other personal characteristics (Cheng, Frith, & Shaw, 2005; Moradi, Dirks, & Matteson, 2005; Muehlenkamp, Swanson, & Brausch, 2005).

Sometimes you may need to provide citations for different parts of a single sentence. No problem. Just add your author and publication date citation within parentheses at every point. It certainly makes for difficult reading to someone not used to APA style, but it's the rule:

> Although objectification is often talked about primarily as something men do to women fueled by research on pornography (McKee, 2005), both men and women objectify (Strelan & Hargreaves, 2005) and can be objectified.

Before we move on, we break for an important warning about one place a very common rookie mistake can be made. Make sure that when you cite a multiple-author piece, you use the exact same order of authorship as found on the first page of the article. *Do not* alphabetize the authors *within* an article. For example, some of the authors of this guide (Schwartz, Landrum, & Gurung, 2012) would be pretty peeved or at least mildly offended if someone cited the book as (Gurung, Landrum, & Schwartz, 2012). Nice alphabetization but not APA style. Alphabetization (by the first author's last name) is key for order of citations and References lists but not for rearranging published author lineups.

What If I Have Two or More Articles by the Same Author and Some Are the Same Year?

Having two or more articles by the same author that were published in the same year can happen more often than you think. People often do a lot of research on similar topics and often have a number of publications on the topic you may want to cite. If you do need to cite **different articles by the same author** and they are all single-author publications, list the author's name once followed by the publication years of the different articles in chronological order from earliest to latest, with a comma between each publication year. If more than one article was published in the same year, then use lowercase letters (e.g., a, b, c) to differentiate the different articles. If the same author has articles with coauthors, add them to the mix in alphabetical order, using the second author's last name to alphabetize the list of sources (if the first two names are the same, then look at the third name, and so on):

> We now know much about how students study and how they should study (Gurung, 2004, 2005a, 2005b; Gurung & McCann, in press; Gurung & Schwartz, 2009).

What If I Have Two or More Articles by Authors With the Same Last Name?

Ever wonder what the citation would look like if Indiana Jones and his father published together? Even when relatives are not working together, this question is often relevant when folks with common last names end up working together. To cite them in the text, use the initials of each author's first and middle name in addition to the last name and publication year:

> It is now clear that drinking a lot of caffeine can be linked to a host of problems (C. R. Smith, 2009; P. T. Smith, 2011).

or

> Both C. R. Smith (2009) and P. T. Smith (2011) have shown that drinking caffeine can be problematic.

How Do I Cite an Article or Document From a Website?

This one is easy as long as you keep website citations to an absolute minimum. There are a few websites that make useful citations. For example, if you want to refer to sociodemographic information (e.g., number of men, women, African Americans, and so on) in a given area, you may want to cite data from the Census Bureau (e.g., U.S. Census Bureau, 2008). That said, if you get the information from a table or figure on a website (even the Census Bureau), there will be a table or figure title that you can cite in-text with the date of publication. The actual organization, website, and source will go into the reference section (see Chapter 10). Also, when you report the year published from a website, you do not report the year that you retrieved the information, but the year that the information was posted to the website. This is difficult to find on many websites and should give you pause about citing that website. If you have to cite it, the format would be to use n.d., which stands for "no date," in parentheses where the year would normally go. Again, there are few other websites that you should be citing (have we said that enough?), but sometimes interesting statistics come in unusual places. For example did you know this little fact?

> In the Midwest, there are more bars than grocery stores, and in Wisconsin there are 5.88 bars per 10,000 people (Zook, 2010).

If I Refer to the Same Article More Than Once in the Same Paragraph Do I Cite It Every Time?

Yes, but not always in the same way. The first time you cite a source in a paragraph you use the style rules described previously. What you do the second time or on subsequent times depends on how you cited it the first time. If you cited a work without putting the author(s) in parentheses the first time, then the **next time** you cite the article, you need not use the publication date. Note the year in the first cite is still in parentheses. An example of this is shown here; the ellipsis indicates an incomplete sentence/quotation:

> Butler and Geis (1990) found that both genders rated men and women leaders equally but treated woman leaders more negatively than they did male leaders. Butler and Geis also found that woman leaders . . .

If your first in-text author citation of the paragraph is inside parentheses, then the subsequent times you cite the same work in the same paragraph you do need to cite the year inside parentheses if you cite the author in the body of the text (yes, we know this may seem silly).

> Studies have found that both genders rate men and women leaders equally but treat woman leaders more negatively than male leaders (Butler & Geis, 1990). Butler and Geis (1990) also found that woman leaders . . .

How Do I Cite an Article That I Read About in Another Article or Book?

Do not (if you can help it) cite a source that you read about in another book or article. Again, we are not asking you to plagiarize but are strongly recommending that you read the original article yourself. It is possible that the article you read (the primary source) that talked about the other article (the secondary source) got it wrong. To some instructors, seeing a secondary source could suggest you did not care enough to go find the original. Why let someone think that of you (it is not true, right)? Importantly, you want to be sure what you write about the secondary source is accurate, and the only way to be sure is to read it yourself. Be especially careful not to use textbooks. Textbooks are great resources and are packed with primary source citations, but they should not substitute for your finding the primary source. If you really must do it (and we are hard-pressed to think of why you would because you can use interlibrary loans or various online full-text databases) your citation looks like this:

> Butler and Geis (as cited in Gurung & Chrouser, 2007) found that both genders rated men and women leaders equally . . .

Which of the references in the preceding example goes into your References list? Actually, only the reference you have before you (the secondary source), which in the example would be Gurung and Chrouser (2007).

How Do I Cite a Lecture, an E-Mail, or a Conversation?

Sometimes you may want to use something incredibly profound that a professor said in class in your paper, or you may want to use information from an e-mail (preferably from an authority on the subject). In some cases, you may even want to cite a person's conversation with you. First off, lectures and conversations are not the best sources for your paper. Don't get us wrong; professors and conversational partners have important things to say and are often accurate and credible, but the gold standard sources for information should be peer-reviewed scientific publications. And no, a lecture is not looked on as a favorable secondary source, although the average lecture often discusses primary sources. If you do have to cite a person, the citation should include the person's initials (separated by periods), followed by the day, month, and year:

> Some of the best ribs are at Oklahoma Joe's in Kansas City (R. E. Landrum, personal communication, June 26, 2010).

That is it. Master these citation styles, and you're well on your way to writing a paper in APA format.

There Is a Method to the Madness 8

When reading about previous research, we are always interested in exactly how the authors collected their data. These details are in the Method section of any APA-style research paper. This section of your APA-style paper comes immediately after your introduction, where you likely have stated your hypothesis in the last paragraph of that section. Mind you, there is a lot more to writing an Introduction, although that is more relevant for a guide on how to write a research paper in general. Introduction and Discussion sections, critical parts of research papers, are not covered in this book because they are not as format heavy as the Method and Results sections. To be honest, we wanted to keep this guide short without sacrificing too much detail.

The Method section is where you take that hypothesis and indicate exactly how you will test your prediction. You need to be sure that the participants you include and the procedure you use actually test your hypothesis. For example, if you predict that test performance will improve when instructors require students to take notes themselves in class rather than receiving the notes from the instructor, your Method section will include how you defined *note taking,* what the instructor's notes included, and finally how you measured test performance. The clear connection needed between your hypothesis and the methods used to test that hypothesis is included within this part of your paper.

Where in the Flow of Pages Do You Place the Method Section?

When it comes to the Method section, we have seen one common mistake— starting a new page in your paper for this section. No new page is needed, and no extra space before the "Method" heading is required. These are the mistakes that students first learning to write in APA style make time and time again. Just keep in mind, "when in doubt, double-space throughout!" The same thing goes for the transition from your Introduction to your Method section, which, by the way, is called the Method section and not the Methods section. Drop the *s*. You can talk about your methods, but you need to write a Method section in your paper. The overall goal of the Method section is to provide enough detail so that another researcher can understand the meaning of what is being studied; better understand the results; and, if needed, replicate your study. The Method section also allows the reader to understand the *generalizability* of your results, which refers to *the extent to which your findings can be applied to other populations and other situations.*

So after you state your hypothesis at the end of your introduction, the Method section will provide the step-by-step playbook with the details about exactly how you tested that hypothesis. As we tell students, the information in this section of the paper should be detailed enough so that the reader can conduct the same experiment to see if the same results are found. You might have learned the term *replicate*, which is exactly what someone is trying to do when using the method from a previous experiment. If you do use the same method as someone else, you can simply include a brief summary of your method and refer the reader to the original source for details. Be careful, though; your instructor might want you to practice writing a Method section "from scratch," even though you borrowed the methodology from another article. However, we are guessing that you likely also learned that direct replication is not usually acceptable in courses in which you are asked to propose original research. After all, originality counts when it comes to design (even though originality clearly is not allowed much when writing in APA style). That said, being aware of past methods used and creating modifications to those methods is a great way to help develop your own research proposals. One of the best ways to become comfortable with APA-style writing is to read as many APA-style publications as you can. One note to remember, however: APA formatting instructions are meant to provide authors a template for how to submit their research for publication to a journal; what actually appears in a journal, format-wise, is quite different from how the author submitted that work to the journal. In other words, there are no published journals in which the article is presented double-spaced, with 1-inch margins on all four sides, and so on.

When writing your own papers, providing the details on how you conducted your research also allows others to evaluate the validity of your experiment. In other words, understanding the details in the Method section about how you collected data can allow readers to figure out if the procedures used really tested the hypothesis in question. So let's say you hypothesize that sleep deprivation leads to a significant drop in test performance—not that we think you are not getting enough sleep (read with a hint of sarcasm . . .). We remember being in college all too well! The Method section will include information such as how much sleep deprivation participants in your experimental group endured, what type of test you had participants take, and how exactly you measured performance. Readers should understand exactly how you operationally defined (in concrete, measureable, and observable terms) sleep deprivation (e.g., 2 hours of sleep or 6 hours of sleep) and how you measured a drop in test performance (e.g., how many tests you used and what type of tests you used). Basically, after reading the Method section of any paper you should know who participated in the study, what they experienced as participants, what materials the authors used, and how the authors defined the independent and dependent variables.

Where Does This Information Go in the Method Section?

APA style requires that you include these details in subsections of the Method section: Subjects or Participants, Apparatus or Materials, and Procedure. Sometimes these subsections are combined depending on how much information you need to include. Sometimes you even see a separate "Design" subsection. We explain when you can combine some of the subsections; we describe what details you should include within each subsection, with an example for each; and we include information on how to format this part of your paper. You didn't think APA would allow you to come up with your own formatting rules, now did you?

Subjects/Participants Subsection

We'll start with the Subjects/Participants subsection. You might be wondering what the difference is between a *subject* and a *participant*. Although APA used to provide specific rules concerning the use of these two terms, according to the sixth edition of the *PM* using either term is acceptable. You need to use only one term for the subheading. Whether you have participants or subjects, this first subsection begins with details about the participants or subjects included in your research.

Many writers start with how many participants were included, followed by the characteristics of your sample relevant to the question at hand. This usually means including demographic information such as age, sex, and ethnic group, but you should include any aspect of your sample that is relevant to why you included these individuals in your research. If you are conducting developmental research, you might want to include the mean age of your participants as well as the age range; whenever you report a mean (or any measure of central tendency), you'll need to report a measure of variability as well—such as range, standard deviation, or standard error. After reading this subsection, a reader should be able to understand why you chose this type of participants in your investigation and why you excluded other types of participants who did not meet your chosen demographic characteristics. Despite the many details you include in this section, you also need to remember to keep the identity of your participants anonymous. Information should be about the group and not about individuals. You cannot state in your Method section that you included the Californian, 18-year-old, Catholic, African American, male with the freckle on his right cheek from the Fall 2010 section of the social psychology course offered at your school. Too much information. A common mistake—if you collected data from students enrolled in an introductory psychology course, new writers want to state that participants were recruited from Introductory Psychology. The reader does not need to know the course name or number in order to replicate your study.

If you include animals as subjects, you need to include information such as the genus, species, and strain of the animals. Also, you need to include the name of the supplier you used to provide the animals. Finally, just as you include demographic information about human participants, similar information is needed when conducting animal research, so include sex, age, weight, and any other relevant information that clearly identifies the type of animal included in the research.

Next, you should include how you recruited your participants. Did you go into introduction to psychology courses; did you use an introductory psychology participation sign-up board or a software program like Experimetrix or Sona Systems; or did you post something on Facebook to recruit for your research? Did you put an ad in the school newspaper asking for volunteers? Did you provide any type of compensation for their participation such as money, course requirement credit, or extra credit? Finally, you need to include information in this section on your *attrition rate*. Attrition refers to the number of participants who began your experiment but who did not finish. Many students ask why attrition rate is important. Why do we need to know how many participants did not complete our experiment? Essentially, students who do not complete the experiment might be different from those who were able to see it through to the end. Often, it is unclear what that difference really is, so simply indicate the number who initially participated in your experiment and the number that completed the experiment.

Typically a participants section includes the following:

- The number of participants/subjects included
- Demographic information about your participants/subjects (e.g., age, sex)
- How you recruited your participants/what supplier was used for your animals
- If participants volunteered or if they were they compensated
- How many participants did not complete your experiment and why

In what follows, we provide an example of a participants section (adapted from Wilson, Stadler, Schwartz, & Goff, 2009, pp. 109–110); also see Chapter 19 and the Participants section in the sample paper written by a psychology major in a research methods course.

Participants

Students enrolled in four introductory psychology courses at three institutions in the southeastern United States participated in this study. The courses were conducted during the summer and fall of 2007. Two female and two male instructors taught the courses, with enrollments between 16 and 40 students each. One hundred and five students were present on the first day of class and were randomly assigned to the experimental conditions and completed surveys. Because 15 students indicated that they had met the teacher previously, their data were removed from the data set for final analyses. Ninety students (72 women and 18 men with an average age of 19.50; $SD = 2.34$) who had no previous experience with the instructor ($n = 82$) or who had met the instructor once during new student orientation ($n = 8$) completed the two surveys at the end of the class period. Ethnicities included 44 Caucasians, 44 non-Caucasian (predominantly African American) students, and two of unknown ethnicity. There were 41 first-year students, 19 sophomore students, 17 junior students, 12 senior students, and one student of unknown classification.

Materials and Apparatus

In this section, you want to tell your readers specifics about the materials or equipment used to collect your data. *Materials* refer to tests, surveys, or questionnaires you used or details of information you presented in paper form or on a computer screen to participants (e.g., the Child Behavior Checklist or the Peabody Picture Vocabulary Test—with appropriate citations included). In comparison, *apparatus* refers to an instrument you might have used to measure reaction time (e.g., a stopwatch) or the equipment used to test an animal's memory for hidden food (e.g., a sand maze). It could also be a specialized computer program that you wrote or some uncommon software you used. Remember, the Method section should let your reader know exactly how you conducted your research, so including the details about the questions asked or the instrument used to measure your dependent variable will be important if indeed someone wants to replicate your study. The amount of detail you include depends on how well-known apparatus or materials are that you're using. If they are well-known, you can simply mention the names for the reader. If they are relatively new and you want to provide a reference where details can be found, you can mention the names for the reader and cite another study that used the same materials and apparatus. If, however, you have come up with an ingenious new way to manipulate your independent variable or measure your dependent measure, then you'll need to include the details.

When can you combine this information with the Procedure subsection? When all your materials are from past studies, consider including a description of your materials in your Procedure subsection. So if the materials in your study are relatively straightforward and well established from previous research, combine the Materials and Procedure subsections into one section. We feel compelled to add here that we do not advise students who are just learning APA style to develop their own measures; that entails a great deal of work before you really know that you have a valid measure. Of course, if there is no measure out there for your dependent variable, then find out what faculty member is most knowledgeable about testing and measurement and all the fun validity and reliability tests that come along with test development. If you are interested in seeing some of the creative equipment used when the science of psychology was a new discipline, check out the following website: http://www3.uakron.edu/ahap/. It's hard to imagine that this equipment was actually used!

Typically, a materials/apparatus section includes the following:

- List of common devices or materials
- Citations for common devices or materials
- Description of uncommon devices or materials
- Why a new measure (e.g., survey) was developed
- Reliability and validity data for the new measure developed

Next, we include an example of a Materials subsection adapted from the same article by Wilson et al. (2009, p. 110), which is a stand-alone Materials section because the researchers developed a survey for their study. You can also take a look in Chapter 19 for a sample of what a Materials section looks like, involving a study where a student created her own survey questions as a measure of the dependent variable.

Materials

A two-page survey was handed to the students as they entered the classroom at the beginning of class period, which they were instructed would be completed in the last 15 min of the class period. On the first page of the survey, students rated statements about their attitudes concerning the instructor (ex. "The instructor seems like an excellent teacher") and the course (ex. "I expect to learn a lot in this course"), on a 5-point Likert-type scale (*Strongly Disagree* to *Strongly Agree*). Three items (opinion of the overall course, opinion of the effectiveness of the instructor, and overall opinion of the instructor) were scored on a 5-point scale from *Poor* to *Excellent*. Questions about the instructor focused on the teaching skills of the instructor, the degree to which the instructor can motivate or interest the students, and the degree to which the instructor likes or cares for the students. Included on the first page of the survey were questions that provided demographic information about the participants (age, gender, ethnicity, year in college, etc.). On the second page of the survey, students indicated their attitudes about touch on a 5-point Likert-type scale (*Strongly Disagree* to *Strongly Agree*). Questions focused on the students' general attitudes about touching (e.g., "Touching is not okay," "Touch is healthy"), their personal preferences about touch (e.g., "I prefer not to be touched often," "I touch people often"), and attitudes about teachers touching students (e.g., "I like it when a teacher touches me," "It is okay for a teacher to touch his/her students"). Three items ("Touching is not okay," "It is not okay to touch people," "I prefer not to be touched often") were reverse-scored when data were entered.

Procedure

This section can start with a sentence or two that tells the reader the design of your experiment. Did you conduct an experiment with manipulated variables, did you use a correlational design, did you use a quasi-experimental design, or did you observe behaviors in a natural setting? This opening statement informs readers of your independent and dependent variables or, if you used a correlational design instead of an experiment, how you assigned participants to the different conditions or groups in your experiment. If you decide to include this information in your procedure section, here is an example of what a design sentence might look like:

> Using a 2 (gender) x 3 (ice cream flavor) mixed factorial design, the order of presentation of ice cream flavors was counterbalanced in an effort to minimize order effects.

Now that you have included the details of who participated and what materials you used to collect data from those participants and the design of your research is clear, it is time for a detailed description of exactly what you did during your experiment. Here is the tricky part. You need to include enough information about details of your procedure that would influence the data collected, but leave out the irrelevant stuff. So you should include information about how you assigned participants to each condition in your research, but you can omit what types of chairs were used where participants sat. Really, after writing this section you should read it (or have someone else read it) to see if the information included allows someone else to conduct the same experiment. The type of detail you need to include really depends on what your research is all about. If you study eyewitness testimony, you will likely not tell your participants that they will need to remember details about an event before the event occurs (we feel compelled at this point to mention the need to follow ethical guidelines when using deception in your research). So if you're not telling your participants that they are about to witness an event they need to remember, what are you telling them? In this case, the specific instructions provided are important for the outcome of your results and therefore you should include them in the procedure section. The rookie mistake (made by someone not reading this book) is again providing too much irrelevant detail. Thus, it is OK to say that you tested students in a lecture hall, but you do not need to say you tested students in the Business Building, Room M204-1. That latter level of detail is irrelevant to the outcome of the study.

Typically, a procedure section includes the following information:

- How you recruited and assigned participants to groups
- What natural observations you made and how you assigned participants to the different groups
- What was your independent variable and how did you manipulate or arrange it
- What your dependent variable was and how you measured it
- Where data collection took place
- How informed consent was achieved, if necessary
- What you informed the participants about the purpose of the research
- What actions the participants performed
- How the researcher was involved in the data collection process
- How long you gave participants to complete the tasks
- How you rewarded participants for their participation
- Whether a debriefing occurred at the conclusion of the study

Once again, using an adaptation from Wilson et al.'s (2009, pp. 110–111) paper for our example, you'll see that when you read the procedure section that follows you will know exactly how data were collected.

Procedure

Before the first day of class, the instructor prepared the two-page survey, folding it in half and taped or stapled it shut. The instructor then made an inconspicuous mark to designate whether the instructor would shake the student's hand before handing the survey to the student. For example, a light pencil stroke was made on the back corner of the survey that was to be given to students with whom the instructor would shake hands.

On the first day of class, the instructor met students as they came into the classroom. As students entered, the instructor greeted the student, using a standard phrase such as "Welcome to the class" or "Welcome, my name is [instructor's name]." At the same time, the instructor either shook the student's hand and handed the survey to the student or simply gave the survey to the student. The student was then instructed not to do anything with the survey until the end of class. Once the time for class arrived, the instructor finished greeting students and proceeded to start class. General first-day-of-class activities occurred—for example, handing out the syllabus, giving an overview of the course, introducing some material. In the last 20 min of class time, the instructor gave instructions to the students about filling out the survey, appointed a student to collect the surveys when everyone had completed them and get the instructor, and then left the room. When the students had completed the survey, and the instructor reentered the classroom, the instructor discussed the study and used it as a tool to introduce research methodology in psychology. Follow-up questions during the discussion indicated that students did not know the nature of the manipulation or the purpose of the study when they were filling out the survey.

Formatting Your Method Section

Now that you know all the information to include in the Method section, and you can write this section so that readers can understand your research, we'll go over the APA rules for formatting this section. We've listed the formatting rules for the Method section below:

- Start the Method section immediately after the end of your introduction.
- Double-space the entire Method section.
- The word **Method** is centered and boldfaced (like your other headings).
- Write the method section using past tense for completed research.
- Each subsection is started on a new line and boldfaced.
- The subsection paragraph begins on a separate line and is indented.

Use the following as a mini-checklist to avoid these commonly found errors:

- Starting the method section on a new page
- Using the heading "Methods" instead of "Method"
- Including extra space between subsections
- Forgetting to boldface headings and subheadings
- Writing the subsection text on the same line as the subsection headings
- Forgetting to use citations for materials borrowed from others
- Not including enough information about the participants or subjects
- Not including enough details about the procedure

When you read any Method section, you should be able to understand who participated in the research, why some participants did not complete the experiment, what was needed in order for the researcher to conduct the investigation, and what exactly the participants did. There should be no question how the data were collected.

And the Winner Is? 9

Writing Your Results and Associated Fun

Analyzing data to solve a mystery can be exciting. Eyes scan the statistical readout searching for that significant p value. Now it is time to share your findings with your instructor and perhaps eventually with others in a poster or paper at a conference or even in a journal article, such as in the *Psi Chi Journal for Undergraduate Research* (www.psichi.org). When it comes to writing your Results section, you will no doubt need to include information about your statistical findings. This chapter will guide you through how to present your statistical information. At times, you will feel like you are writing in a foreign language. Hang in there; we will help you make sense and let you know how and when to use all the new words and symbols you're learning.

The first question to ask yourself when writing your Results section is, "Should I include my findings in a table or figure, or should I include them all in my Results section?" The general rule of thumb is to present your data in a Results paragraph if you have three or fewer sets of numbers. So if you are reporting statistics for three or fewer groups (i.e., means, standard deviations, sample size for each) you can write the Results section without a table. If you are able to write a sentence that flows well and make sense, then leave the information in the paragraph. The best way to test the flow of a sentence is to read the sentence out loud. If it sounds like too much information to include in one sentence, then it likely is, and you should consider using a figure or a table. Typically, you create a table when you have four or more sets of numbers. Remember, if you present your means and additional statistics within a table or figure, you should not also include those numbers within your text. That would be statistics overkill. What you do need to do is tell readers in the Results section where they can find your data (e.g., which table or figure) and what they will find there when they turn to that page. For example, if you included the means and standard deviations for each of the eight different groups of your experiment, you might write this:

Descriptive statistics for all groups appear in Table 1.

Again, you want to be sure to tell readers what information they will find when they read over the table you are asking them to look at so they can better understand your results. Take a look at Chapter 13 for details on using figures and tables in your paper. In that chapter, we cover all the APA formatting issues, and believe us, there are specific ways that APA wants you to present your findings in tables and figures.

Let's Talk Statistics

When including the type of statistic you conducted in your Results section, there is no need to provide a **reference** for the commonly used analyses (e.g., *t* tests, multiple regressions). Few (if any) readers will be excited to go find that reference and spend an evening reading all about commonly used inferential statistics. To be fair, there are some pretty exciting books that cover the treatments of statistics using SPSS, a common statistical package. One of our favorites is Field (2010), a real hoot to read (and you think we are kidding?). There are three reasons why you should consider a reference with your statistic, and you will likely need to be concerned only with the first reason we include here. If your paper topic is focused on a particularly obscure type of statistic, you need to include a reference. References for statistics are also needed. Or if you use a common statistic in a most unusual way, a reference should be included. But we usually discourage our students from using or creating new and unusual statistics for their research, so it is unlikely you will need a reference for that reason.

These same rules apply to formulas. There is no need to include the formulas for common statistics such as a *t* test or a mean. But when you start to use those newfangled, never-before-heard-of statistics, then by all means, present your equations. Now, if you counter that you have never heard of most statistics before, we counter-counter that we mean the statistics not commonly seen in published journal articles. We are guessing that you will not be likely to include any newfangled formulas when you are just learning how to write in APA style. For that matter, many researchers who are well versed in APA style are not creating newfangled formulas either.

All that said, the important question is how to **present your statistics** within the Results section of your paper. (Note: for tips on writing the Results section in general, check out Landrum, 2008.) Having taught research methods, we know that presenting one's results is often a difficult task for students to learn at first, but we can tell you that once students grasp the way this section is formatted, most future Results sections are a snap. The important idea to keep in mind is that you need to write this section of your paper so that the reader can understand exactly what you found when you ran your statistical analyses. For example, you need to write about the groups you compared and the results from each group, and you need to know your means, standard deviations, and effect sizes. In other instances, you may need to report the correlations, sample sizes, effect sizes, or power analyses. The type of numbers presented really depends on the type of statistics you have performed and the complexity of your design. Here is an example from a Results section (Gurung & Chrouser, 2007):

> There was a significant, positive correlation between scores of both the objectification of the models and self-objectification, $r(81) = .64$, $p < .001$, indicating that individuals who objectify themselves also show a tendency to objectify others and vice versa. Interestingly, self-esteem showed significant, positive relationships with objectification tendency, $r(81) = .24$, $p = .007$, and self-objectification, $r(81) = .29$, $p = .001$

Notice in the examples that follow, you typically include the statistical information after a comma at the end of the sentence, and when you write about the means within your text, you use the words and not the symbols. You would write "The mean of the experimental group was significantly greater" and not "The M of the experimental group. . . ." The symbols are used when reporting the means within parentheses (see Table 9.1 for the most common symbols used).

> **Incorrect:** The M for children using the drawing technique was 72% and was not significantly different than the Ms for children in the verbal condition at 70%, $F(1, 48) = 1.45$, $p = .09$.

> **Correct:** Children's reports when using the drawing technique ($M = 72\%$, $SD = 0.45$) were not significantly more accurate than children's reports when asked to just tell us what they could remember without drawing ($M = 70\%$, $SD = 1.89$), $F(1, 48) = 1.45$, $p = .09$.

Basics and Beyond

One of the more complicated rules when writing an APA-style Results section is knowing whether to use standard, **boldface**, or *italicized* typeface. Typically, the type of statistics you will include should be italicized. So when writing about how many participants you included in your experiment, you use an uppercase, italicized N. You switch to a lowercase italicized n when writing about a subset of that number (e.g., how many participants were in your experimental group). See Table 9.1 adapted from a similar table presented in the *PM*.

If by chance you are including statistics that involve vectors or matrices (and we doubt that will be the case), then you would type those symbols in **boldface.** You might need to include a symbol for Greek letters (e.g., β for Beta), subscripts (e.g., H_0 for null hypothesis), or superscripts (e.g., r^2 for r squared). Those symbols—Greek

Table 9.1 Typical Statistical Symbols and Abbreviations

Symbol or Abbreviation in English	Meaning of Symbol or Abbreviation
ANOVA	Analysis of variance
ANCOVA	Analysis of covariance
CI	Confidence interval
d	Cohen's measure of effect size
d'	Discriminability, sensitivity measure
df	Degrees of freedom
ES	Effect size
f	Frequency
f_e	Expected frequency
f_o	Observed frequency
F	F distribution
GLM	Generalized linear model
H_0	Null hypothesis
H_1 (or H_a)	Alternative hypothesis
HSD	Tukey's honestly significant difference
M (or $\bar{X}$)	Sample mean
MANOVA	Multivariate analysis of variance
MANCOVA	Multivariate analysis of covariance
Mdn	Median in the sample
MS	Mean square
MSE	Mean square error
n	A part of the sample population
N	Total number in the sample
ns	Not statistically significant
p	Probability
r	Pearson's correlation coefficient
r^2	Estimate of the Pearson product-moment correlation squared

(Continued)

Table 9.1 (Continued)

Symbol or Abbreviation in English	Meaning of Symbol or Abbreviation
r_s	Spearman rank order correlation
R	Multiple correlation
R^2	Multiple correlation squared; measure of strength of association
SD	Standard deviation
SE	Standard error
SS	Sum of squares
t	Student's t distribution; a statistical test based on the Student t distribution; the sample value of the t-test statistic
z	A standardized score; the value of a statistic divided by its standard error

Symbol or Abbreviation in Greek	Meaning of Symbol or Abbreviation
α	Alpha (probability of making a Type I Error)
β	Beta (probability of making a Type II Error)
η^2	Eta squared (effect size)
μ	Population mean
ρ	Population product-moment correlation
σ	Standard deviation (for the population)
σ^2	Variance
χ^2	Chi-square distribution
Σ	Summation
Φ	Phi (effect size for chi-square distributions)
θ	Omega (effect size for meta-analysis)

letters, subscripts, or superscripts that are not variables—are typed in standard type. Now, to make things even more complicated, the APA *PM* reminds us that all other test statistics are italicized (e.g., *t* and *F*). Again, check out Table 9.1, which illustrates some of the most commonly used test statistics and abbreviations.

Formatting Your Results Paragraph

Once you figure out what language to use when writing about your statistics, keep a few basic rules in mind. First, when writing out mathematical formulas, include spaces in your mathematical copy. In other words, treat each number as if it were a separate word. Don't forget to include punctuation after equations. This is true whether an equation is in a paragraph or standing all alone.

Incorrect: $1+3=4$

Correct: $1 + 3 = 4.$

Most equations should fit nicely on one line and are easy to include in your text. When you need to include fractions, just use a slash ("/") to present the numerator over the denominator. When you need to include a more complicated equation (e.g., one that requires a square root of a fraction), then you'll need to display it on its very own line.

Incorrect: $\frac{3}{4}$

Correct: 4/5

Finally (and we promise this is the last part), when you are writing about percentages, APA style states that you use the % symbol when preceded by a number (e.g., 10%); otherwise use the word *percentage* (e.g., "a large percentage of the sample"). Note: Use the word *percent* only when it follows a number that must be spelled out (e.g., at the beginning of a sentence); don't use it in place of *percentage.*

Incorrect: Less than 10 percent of the sample reported wearing protective clothing.

Correct: Less than 10% of the sample reported wearing protective clothing.

Incorrect: A large percent of the sample reported wearing protective clothing.

Correct: A large percentage of the sample reported wearing protective clothing.

Greek letters, subscripts, and superscripts that aren't variables are in standard type, symbols for vectors and matrices are in bold, and statistical symbols are in italics (APA, 2010a, p. 118). If something serves as both an abbreviation and a symbol, look at Table 4.5 (pp. 119–123) of the APA *PM.* The fine print on page 123 informs us that if a form is used as both an abbreviation and a symbol, use the abbreviation form when referring to the concept and the symbol form for a specific number.

Including Effect Size and Power

For many undergraduate research assignments, especially those completed within a single semester, sample sizes are often not very large. As a result, there is also an unfortunate shortage of significant findings. When faced with statistical tests that are not significant, you may erroneously conclude that you've wasted your time. But wait; statistical significance is influenced by two major factors: sample size and effect size. If the number of students in your study is very large, this large sample size can make even small statistical differences significant. By the same token, if you have a very small sample, then you may not get a statistically significant difference *even though there may be differences between groups.* Not finding statistical significance with a very small sample could just mean the research study could not detect the existing difference (Gurung & Schwartz, 2009). This is where the size of your effect comes in handy.

Effect sizes are valuable statistics that provide the reader with a sense of the importance of your research results. Essentially, this statistic indicates the strength of the relationship between your variables. So in addition to knowing if the relationship is significant, readers are interested in knowing the strength of the relationship. Correspondingly, including the effect size in your Results section is now an explicit recommendation of the APA *PM* (APA, 2010a). The key is that the size of the effect provides an idea of the real-world significance of the finding. Researchers use a benchmark established by Cohen (1988), who categorized effect sizes of .20 as small, .50 as medium, and .80 as large. In most psychological research, an effect size of .20 is something to be taken very seriously. Even a small effect size can have large real-world implications (the effect of aspirin reducing heart attacks has an effect size of only .06; Bloom & Lipsey, 2004).

Effect sizes are available for most statistics directly in the statistical programs (e.g., SPSS) and are represented by the letter *d*. The *PM* also strongly recommends the use of confidence intervals (CIs), a measure of the precision of your statistic, also available in the statistics program. The effect size and confidence interval follow your reporting of the *p* value. Like all statistics in APA style, the letter *d* is in italics. Here is what it would look like in a Results section from a study by Prestwich, Perugini, and Hurling (2010, pp. 45–46):

> In a surprise recall task at Time 2, those in the implementation intention + plan reminder condition showed greater plan recall than those in the implementation intention + goal reminder condition, $t(84) = 5.09$, $p < .001$, $d = 1.10$, 95% CI [0.63, 1.62], supporting Hypothesis 4.

The 80s rock band the Police sang, "Murder by numbers, 1 2 3, it's as easy to learn as your ABCs." Not murder by any means, but statistics can be intimidating. The neat outcome is that if you learn to write them well, you will have an easier time reading Results sections as well. Then the fun really starts as those mazes of numbers all make sense and research really comes to life. Have fun.

Everybody Needs References 10

A Helpful Note

In the new APA *PM* (APA, 2010a), there are 77 different examples of reference formats. Providing 77 different examples in this chapter would be overwhelming. Frankly, many of the rules in the *PM* will not be needed when first learning how to write in APA style. This section is a great example of working on a "need-to-know basis." There are a small number of commonly used reference sources. These are the ones we feature. We believe the number of details included in the *PM* can overwhelm most students, and therefore we downplay them. By sticking to the basics, we try to minimize the confusing exceptions and details. With each example, we have listed the basic components of that type of reference, allowing you to see the differences between each type of source you are likely to cite. However, we wanted to be up front and let you know that we've included the type of references that are *most likely* to be those you need to include in your paper. If you feel compelled to know those extra details, we are confident you know where to look.

Creating Your Reference Section

When writing about that very interesting topic you chose for your paper, undoubtedly you took a look at the past research related to your subject matter in order to make sure your great idea for an experiment or a term paper had not already been completed by someone else. As we presented in Chapter 5, when you include information from any of those other sources, you are immediately in need of a reference list section for your paper. You must include most of the items you cite in your paper in your reference list. This way, interested readers who want to take a look at one of the sources you used will have all the information needed to get that source on their own. Think of your reference list as an indication of your academic pedigree; you get to show off your skills in locating sources and analyzing what is relevant and what is not. Your References section recreates the intellectual journey you took to draw the conclusions you made in your paper.

Most of the sources you include in your reference list will be journal articles, books, or chapters from books. We also recognize that you found many of your sources through electronic searches. So we have included a section to cover how to reference those as well. Luckily, if you cited a personal communication in your paper (and we don't recommend you do so unless necessary), you don't need to include it in your reference list (that is why we said "most" earlier)—though we know that Aunt Susan, who discussed the importance of communication in any relationship, will be upset that she was not given the recognition deserved in your paper. Remember, you need to include only the sources you cited in your paper (i.e., this is not a bibliography containing a list of every item you researched). One common mistake we have found that our students make is to include a reference they read because it was related to their topic but in the end was not included in their paper. Sometimes, this error occurs because students worked on a number of drafts of their paper, and during that time deleted some information (and a citation or two . . . or three) that included sources they had listed in the reference section earlier—yet another good reason for proofreading!

One easy way to see if all the sources you have cited are in the reference list and that all the sources listed in your reference list are in fact cited in your paper is to search for each first author's name in the reference list using the "Find" function in Word (see the screen shot of the header bar that appears on the screen in Word 2007, or in any version of Word use the keyboard shortcut Ctrl+F). The Find function is circled on the right of the header. Simply type in any word or name and Word will search for that word or name throughout your document. For a more low-tech solution, just print a paper copy and hand check each citation in the text with each source listed in the reference section. Make sure every citation in the text has a corresponding reference—and that name spellings, publication dates, and page numbers (for quotations or specific pages you want the reader to see in the source you're citing) match between a citation and its reference; likewise, make sure every entry in the References section is located and cited properly in the text somewhere. Finally, one more common mistake is changing the order of authors in a reference to alphabetical order in the citation of that reference. Always make sure you use the same author order in your citation as listed in the source. We mentioned this in an earlier chapter but believe it is worthwhile to mention it again here. The order of authors' names is something one should never change because usually that order is determined by each author's contribution to the research.

Let's get to the reason why you turned to this chapter. How do you put together a reference list? The reference list is the part of the paper that makes you realize APA style is really different from other styles of writing. So if you are used to writing papers for an English, history, or chemistry course, get ready to learn some new rules. There are *very* specific rules you need to follow. In our many years of teaching students how to write in APA style, we have found that some of the biggest APA style challenges occur when attempting to create a list of references. This is likely because of the specific rules for each of the different types of sources. The good news is that the rules, though abundant, are very specific. You can nail them, especially with our help. The bad news is that there are many details and ways to make mistakes when creating a list of your references. This is a part of your paper where you have to pay special attention to detail.

Using Abbreviations

For many of the references we describe subsequently, you will need to include information in the form of an abbreviation. Many abbreviations are used in this section, some of which are standard abbreviations (e.g., state names). Additional abbreviations are not as commonly used. To help clarify what abbreviations to use, we've included Table 10.1. For more on abbreviations see Chapter 16.

Table 10.1 Using Abbreviations in Your References Section	
The Term	**The Abbreviation for the Term in Your Reference List (With Accompanying Punctuation)**
Digital object identifier	doi:
Edition	(2nd ed.).
Editor	(Ed.).
Editors	(Eds.). or (Eds.),
Revised edition	(Rev. ed.).
No date	(n.d.).
Page (for a chapter in a book)	(p. 18).
Pages (for a chapter in a book)	(pp. 194–201)
Third edition	(3rd ed.).
Volume	(Vol. 3),
Volumes	(Vols. 1–3)

The Basics

To simplify this part of APA style, we'll start by listing the basic components, a couple of examples, and the basic rules for formatting this part of your paper. Then we present some of the more detailed rules based on the type of source you want to include in the reference list. We'll warn you now: It is in the details about the different types of sources that the rules start to get more complicated. So once we cover the very basics, we include examples of the most common types of references you are likely to use when first learning how to write in APA style. **HINT:** When using the examples below, pay attention to the placement of punctuation (e.g., commas and periods) and pay attention to what is in *italics*. For each source listed in your reference list, APA format has rules on when to use a comma and when to use a period as well as additional rules on what part of the reference should be italicized.

The basic components of most citations placed in your reference list are these:

- Alphabetize your list of references using the first author's last name. Only the initials of the authors' first and middle names are included (i.e., do not write out the full first name), and there is a space between the initials. For a work with multiple authors, a comma separates each author's name (even when there are only two authors).
- For a work with multiple authors, an ampersand (&) is used before the last author's name, with a comma before the ampersand.
- The order of authors for any work listed as a reference should never be changed from the order listed on the first page of the article (i.e., never alphabetize multiple authors *within* a single reference).
- Date of publication (the real date of publication—not the date that you found it—especially pertinent for any citations based on information retrieved from the Internet) is placed within parentheses followed by a period.
- Title of the work follows the date of publication.
- The entire reference is prepared using a hanging indent and is double-spaced.

Journal Article

Now on to the details that are determined by the type of source you're including in your References. Let's start with a journal article, which is the most common type of reference you'll be expected to use. This is an example of a journal article:

Gurung, R. A. R., Ansburg, P. I., Alexander, P. A., Lawrence, N. K., & Johnson, D. E. (2008). Scholarship of teaching and learning strategies and tactics: The state of the scholarship of teaching and learning in psychology. *Teaching of Psychology, 35,* 249–261. doi:10.1080/00986280802374203

In this example for a journal article notice the following:

- Both the title of the article and the title of the journal are included.
- The only words capitalized in the title are the first word and the first word after the colon. If there are any proper nouns in the title, those proper nouns are always capitalized.
- Except for the conjunctions (e.g., *and, or*), and short prepositions (e.g., *at, as, of*), or articles (e.g., *an, the)*, all the first letters of major words (i.e., longer than 3 letters) in the periodical title are capitalized.
- The title of the journal is italicized.
- The volume number is included and italicized.
- The issue number of the volume is *not* included, which is true in most cases because most journals are not paginated by issue.
- The page numbers of the journal article are included. Note that inclusive page numbers are followed by a period (without including "pp.").
- The publisher's name is *not* included for journal articles.
- The doi (digital object identifier) number is included (list it whenever available, whether you got the article online or in printed form).

Book

At times, you will want to include information found in a book rather than a journal article. When you do this, keep in mind the important difference between primary and secondary sources, as discussed earlier in this chapter. A book is a great source for a review of a topic, but you'll need to get the actual journal articles discussed in the book to really understand what the research entailed AND to include it in your paper as a primary source.

If we change the example to a reference for a **book**, you'll notice some of the basics remain along with some changes:

Schwartz, B. M., Landrum, R. E., & Gurung, R. A. R. (2012). *An easyguide to APA style*. Thousand Oaks, CA: Sage.

- The book title is italicized.
- The only words capitalized in a book title are the first word, the first word after a colon, and proper nouns.
- The book title is followed by a period.
- The publisher's location is included (city and state abbreviation), followed by a colon, and then the name of the publisher.
- A period is placed after the publisher's name.
- If the author and publisher are the same, place the publisher where the author is listed and use the word *Author* where you would include the publisher.

Chapter in an Edited Book

Instead of citing an entire book, you might want to cite just a **chapter in a book.** In this example, the chapter is in an edited book, which means the chapters are written by different authors, and the book was edited by one or more individuals. The reference would look like this:

Halpern, D. F. (1999). The war of the worlds: Why psychology helps bridge the gap between students' and professors' conceptual understanding. In B. A. Pescosolido & R. Aminzade (Eds.), *The social worlds of higher education: Handbook for teaching in a new century* (pp. 91–94). Thousand Oaks, CA: Pine Forge Press.

In this example, for a chapter in a book, notice the following changes to the reference:

- The author(s) of the chapter are listed first.
- The title of the chapter is included after the date of publication.
- The editors of the book are listed with their initials before their last names.
- After the editor's name you include the abbreviation (Ed.), followed by a comma.
- A period is placed after the abbreviation for editor.
- The title of the chapter is *not* italicized.
- The title of the book is italicized.
- The only words capitalized in each title are the first words and the first words after a colon.

Online Sources

Fortunately, many sources for your paper are available through a few taps on your keyboard without ever having to get up from where you are. We won't discuss here how fortunate you are to have these online resources because we are confident you've heard from many of your professors all about the days when we had to actually go the library to read past research or wait for days or even weeks for the library to receive an interlibrary loan from another college or university before we could even read the article. APA quickly became aware that many of our print sources are accessed online and many additional sources are available only online. Consequently, more APA rules were created on how to cite and reference these documents.

You should notice that most of the same information included in the reference for a source is needed when you access the article or book online. When you find the book or article online, present most of the source information in the same order as in the reference. The part of the source information that we need to add for these electronic resources is either the URL (uniform resource locator) or the doi. Online information can be moved; we've all experienced typing in a URL only to receive a message that the information can no longer be accessed there. As a result, many sources now have a doi that will not be affected if the source is moved to another site; however, not all publishers include a doi. We expect more and more sources to have a doi, so knowing how to include these sources in your reference section will become more and more relevant. To find a doi, look at the source information listed online with most articles or in the upper-right corner of an online version of a printed article. At times, "doi" will appear before the numbers; other times, you'll find a long list of numbers (and sometimes letters) that start with the numbers *1* and *0* (10). One general rule of thumb to keep in mind: When a book or article is available only online, you substitute the publisher information with the online retrieval information (see examples for details). Some of your sources will have just the URL, and some will have both a URL and a doi. We provide examples for all of these possibilities.

If you obtained an **electronic** version of a paper that is available in a printed version, you include it as follows:

Reaser, A., Prevatt, F., Petscher, Y., & Proctor, B. (2007). The learning and study strategies of college students with ADHD. *Psychology in the Schools, 44,* 627–638. doi:10.1002/pits.20252

Notice the following about the reference with the doi:

- Most of the parts of the reference are the same as for the printed source.
- doi is printed in lowercase letters.
- There is no period at the end of the series of doi numbers.
- There is no space after the colon following doi.

The following is an example of an online source using a URL but without a doi:

Wilson, J. H., Stadler, J. R., Schwartz, B. M., & Goff, D. M. (2009). Touching your students: The impact of a handshake on the first day of class. *Journal of the Scholarship of Teaching and Learning, 9,* 108–117. Retrieved from http://academics.georgiasouthern.edu/ijsotl/v4n1.html

Notice the following about the reference with the URL:

- The reference includes the same basic information as in other references.
- You include the words "Retrieved from" before the URL.
- Retrieval dates are needed only for material that changes over time.
- A period *does not* occur at the end of a URL.
- The URL is not in a blue font, nor is it underlined; you will need to use the "remove hyperlink" function in Word to format this properly (either right-click on the URL and select *Remove hyperlink* or select the URL and

press Ctrl+Shift+F9; to quickly remove all hyperlinks in the same file, press Ctrl+A to select the entire document, and then press Ctrl+Shift+F9 to deactivate the hyperlinks).

Articles With Seven or More Authors

Though you will typically find that most of your articles and books are written by a smaller group of authors, you might come across a source that includes more than seven authors. You might recall reading about these details in the chapter on citations, where we discuss how to cite and reference articles with different numbers of authors. Most of the reference format with this many authors is exactly the same as we've described already. However, because the APA *PM* added a new rule in the sixth edition, we want to make sure you are aware of how to include this type of source in your References section.

When a reference has seven or fewer authors, you can include **all** the authors' names in the reference list. However, for articles with more than seven authors, you include the first six authors' names, followed by three spaced periods (an ellipsis), and then the last author's name. (HINT: Try not to be an author whose name comes after the sixth author's unless you are the last author on a research team; otherwise, you'll never see your name appear in a reference list.) Next are two examples of this type of reference; the first example is a print version, and the second example is an online version (with 17 authors; we kid you not).

Halonen, J. S., Bosack, T., Clay, S., McCarthy, M., Dunn, D. S., Hill, G. W., IV, . . . & Whitlock, K. (2003). A rubric for learning, teaching, and assessing scientific inquiry in psychology. *Teaching of Psychology, 30,* 196–208.

Lennertz, L., Grabe, H. J., Ruhrmann, S., Rampacher, F., Vogeley, A., Schulze-Rauschenbach, S., . . . & Wagner, M. (2010). Perceived parental rearing in subjects with obsessive–compulsive disorder and their siblings. *Acta Psychiatrica Scandinavica, 121,* 280–288. doi:10.1111/j.1600–0447.2009.01469

Conference Presentations

We often tell our students that the most up-to-date research is found at conferences where researchers present their findings before publishing them in a journal or a book. Keep in mind, often if you e-mail researchers known for research in a specific area, they will share these presentations with you. To include this in your reference section, the sources would appear as follows:

Schwartz, B. M., Tatum, H. E., Coffey, C. C., & Mandarakas, A. (2010, August). *Classroom interactions: The influence of gender of professor and gender of student.* Poster presentation at the annual meeting of the American Psychological Association, San Diego, CA.

Tatum, H. (2007, August). Barbie, Goldilocks, and other stories for the psychology of gender. In B. M. Schwartz (Chair), *Using stories from our personal lives to teach psychological theories and concepts.* Symposium presented at the annual convention of the American Psychological Association, San Francisco, CA.

This illustrates a poster presentation at a conference in the first example and a paper presented as part of a symposium at a conference in the second example. In these types of reference, notice the following:

- Following the year, the month of the presentation is included within the parentheses.
- For the poster presentation, **italicize the title of the presentation** and indicate that the research was a poster presentation **at** a conference.
- For the paper presented **at** a symposium, the chair of the symposium is included, first initial and last name followed by the word "Chair" in parentheses.
- **The title of a presentation at a symposium follows the year and month and is not italicized;** instead, the title of the symposium is italicized.
- **For both poster presentations and papers presented at a symposium,** the **name** of the convention and its **location** are included.

Newspapers and Magazines

We are confident that you will hear from your professors that if at all possible, avoid including sources of information from newspapers and magazines. Instead, find the reference cited in that newspaper or magazine and find the original source of the information discussed in the article. Some of the time, the newspaper and magazine articles report about the primary source (see also Chapter 7 on citing sources). Primary sources are the articles or books that present the original text by the author of the investigation. In contrast, secondary sources refer to articles or books that discuss another article and the findings from that source. For example, let's say we discuss information in our paper that we read about in one article, a primary source we will call Source A. We would include Source A in our References. As you read Source A, you will likely find information about another related study, which we will call Source B. Again Source B is called a secondary source if we do not actually find the article and read it (and that would not be a good idea). However, if you are unable to read Source B yourself and you really want to include information in your paper about Source B, then you would need to cite where you read about Source B, which in this case would mean Source A. You do not include Source B in your References. In this example, you have read the Gurung and Schwartz (2009) chapter, in which they discuss Hattie's work. However, you never read Hattie's work directly from his book.

Hattie's (as cited in Gurung & Schwartz, 2009) work on visible learning makes an important contribution to the literature.

Notice that you include the author for the secondary source and the primary source, but you do not include the year for the primary source. The year is included only for the secondary source.

Should you find that you are unable to access the primary source, the following are examples of reference items when the information is obtained from a magazine and newspaper article.

Goldstein, R. (2010, March). Major developments in undergraduate psychology. *Observer, 23*(3), 23–26.

West, K. (2010, February 2). Some odd thoughts about thinking. *The News and Advance*, pp. B1, B3.

Notice a few things about these examples: Most magazines start with page 1, so the issue number needs to be included if available. Many articles in newspapers are on multiple pages in specific sections of the paper. Include the exact pages of the article's location and include the section as well.

Basic Reference Section Formatting Rules

Next, we fill you in on some of the basic reference list formatting rules (e.g., headings, margins, order of references). We have noted all these rules on the sample reference page included in Chapter 19.

- Start your reference list on a separate page at the end of your paper.
- Place the reference list before any footnotes, tables, figures, or appendices.
- Use 1-inch margins for top, bottom, left, and right sides of the page.
- Center the word "References" at the top of the page.
- Double-space your references with no extra line space between each reference. (See Chapter 14 on how to make sure these extra spaces are not included.)
- Use hanging indents (and set it up in Word rather than using a hard return and spaces or tabs)—first line for each reference starts at the margin and all other lines are indented about 1/2 inch (in Microsoft Word, highlight the reference, and hit Ctrl+T).
- Alphabetize the list by the first author's last name.
- Use each author's full last name and only initials for their first and middle names.
- Italicize the title of the work.
- Start with one-author works and earliest publication year when you include multiple sources with the same first author.

- When you have sources with the same first author and same year of publication, place lowercase letters after the year (e.g., 2009a). The articles are ordered according to how they are alphabetized by title in the reference list. For example, when you have two sources by different authors with the same last name (e.g., Schwartz, B. and Schwartz, R.), alphabetize by the initials of the author's first name.
- Include all authors listed for each source, up to seven names total (see the section in this chapter titled "Articles With Seven or More Authors").

Some of the Not-So-Basic Rules You Might Need

- When no author's name is included, alphabetize using the first word of the article or book title or the first word of the organizational title.
- When no date of publication is available, use n.d. (for no date) in parentheses directly following the authors' names.
- As a general guideline, in every APA reference citation format, some part of the citation will be italicized.

By now, you recognize that the reference section of your paper is by far the most complicated when it comes to using APA style. And as stated at the beginning of this chapter, this summary of details is only the tip of the iceberg; our goal here is to present the most commonly used sources in an attempt to avoid what is often overwhelming in the *PM* (i.e., a list of 77 different types of references). APA provides guidelines on how to reference everything from a map to a video blog post to a letter from a private collection. However, our experiences with teaching students how to write in APA style have taught us what sources students typically use when writing their papers. Those are the sources we included in this chapter. Should you need to cite a more uncommon source such as a court decision, a patent, or an archival source with a corporate author, you are just going to have to go find a copy of that *PM.*

SECTION IV

Presenting Your Work in APA Format

The Numbers Game 11

How to Write Numbers (and When the Rules Change)

When writing an APA-style paper, you'll need to know information pertaining to how to express numbers, which could mean writing *10, 11,* and *12,* or *ten, eleven,* and *twelve.* In fact, numbers are everywhere in APA-style writing. Whether you are writing how many participants you included in your experiment, how old the participants were, the dosage of a drug used, or what percentage of a population demonstrated a behavior, you'll need to know how to properly include that information in your paper. You won't be surprised to find out that the APA *PM* has specific guidelines on this matter with *many* exceptions to those guidelines. The big distinction here is whether to use numerals (e.g., *15*) or words (e.g., *fifteen*) to express numbers. We've included a table at the end of the chapter that allows you to look up the type of number notation you need to include and how to express that number (see Table 11.1). In that table, you'll also find examples for each rule. Keep in mind when using the table that you should look for the specific type of number you want to include by skimming the far left-hand column. It starts with the very general rule and moves to more specific rules. The rules that follow apply when writing with both ordinal (e.g., 12th grade) and cardinal numbers (e.g., the 12 seniors). You use ordinal numbers when the number refers to rank or order (e.g., the first grade). On the other hand, use cardinal numbers to indicate the number of something (e.g., 40 participants).

When You Use Numerals

So what is the general rule for numbers in APA style? Good question, because you'll likely find that APA rules for numbers are different from the rules you use when writing papers in other disciplines, such as when using MLA for an English literature paper. Too often, students find that out the hard way. So we are going to help you avoid the dreaded red ink and/or tracked changes/comments on your APA-style paper.

The general rule of thumb is to use numerals (10, 11, 12, etc.) for numbers 10 and over. Did you notice that we used the numeral *10* and not the word *ten*? Yup. We followed APA style. So if you're reviewing the methodology used in past research and you need to write in your paper, "We gave participants 18 vignettes to review," you express the number as a numeral. However, if the participants were given only eight vignettes, you now need to use the word *eight* instead.

Incorrect: We presented all participants with ten different questionnaires.

Correct: We presented all participants with 10 different questionnaires.

You might be thinking, "That's simple enough. Numerals for 10 and over; words for under 10!" Not so fast. There are times when you use numerals regardless of the number. For instance, when you are writing your **Abstract**, you use numerals only. Yea! One place to not have to stop and think about number rules.

When the number immediately precedes a **unit of measurement**, use a numeral. For example, "The rats received 500 mg of Prozac. The rats in the control group receiving 0 mg were envious of those in the experimental group." So when your research includes information about number of yards, inches, pounds, milliseconds, lumens, hertz, and the list can go on and on . . . you should include a numeral before the unit. By the way, there are entirely separate rules for how to abbreviate units of measurement, such as inches, pounds, and seconds. See our tips in Chapter 16 on how to present units of measurement correctly.

Incorrect: The rats received five-hundred mg of Prozac. The rats in the control group receiving zero mg were envious of those in the experimental group.

Correct: The rats received 500 mg of Prozac. The rats in the control group receiving 0 mg were envious of those in the experimental group.

When writing about your results, you might need to write about **mathematical functions**—statistics, quantities, ratios, percentiles, or quartiles, for example. In that case, you need to stick to the numerals. Using numerals is relevant for your Results section because that is where you include all your statistical results. You might come across these numbers when discussing prevalence of a behavior, in which case you would write, for example, "Less than 9% of the population agreed with the local election results" (see Chapter 9 of this book for more details about writing your Results section).

Here is an easy rule to follow. When you include numbers in **graphs**, and this is common, you use only numerals and not words. You've likely come across bar graphs that include the mean score presented above each bar; that number would be expressed as a numeral.

Research papers often include information about parts of a **numbered series**. You might need to refer to "Chapter 3" in a book or "Table 4" in your paper. This is another exception to the rule and you need to use a numeral. Your paper might also include a list of items. When the series of items are separate paragraphs, then each item is preceded by a numeral that is followed by a period (e.g., 1.). In this case parentheses are not used to enclose the number. However, when the series is within a sentence or a paragraph, you don't use a number at all. Instead, your list includes a series of letters (e.g., "The following insects were presented to each participant: (a) ants, (b) bugs, (c) spiders, and (d) moths"). This type of ordered listing is called seriation, and we tackle it in Chapter 15.

The exceptions to the rule do not end there (see Table 11.2 for a list of all exceptions). When a number represents time, dates, ages, scores, points on a scale, or exact sums of money, use numerals. For example, "The participants were 3- to 4-year-olds." Regardless of how young or old your participants are, use numerals to express their age. You will likely include in your procedure section information about the length of time your experiment required (e.g., 3 hr 47 min), and you might also include the time of day when your conducted your research (e.g., at 3:12 p.m.). Finally, if you are fortunate enough to have funds to compensate your participants, you would express the exact sum of money offered using numerals and write, "All participants received $8 for participating." Of course, APA style would not be complete without an exception to this exception, and this brings us to the next section of this chapter.

When You Use Words

There are times when you are writing a research proposal and do not have exact time information. In those cases when you must write **approximations**, you need to use words rather than numerals. In this case, you would write "Participants returned to the laboratory for Session 2 approximately ten days following their first visit." This is the first of several rules that requires you to use words to express numbers rather than numerals.

APA style suggests that you **don't start a sentence** with a number (e.g., "Ninety-six percent accuracy ratings emerged for the group that received the study guide."). However, when you feel the need to do so (and you never know when that need will emerge), you always use words to express those numbers (rather than using numerals). But perhaps that exception to the rule should be avoided, and you should just not start sentences with numbers.

The same rule also applies to **titles** and **headings**. Those numbers at the beginning of titles and headings would be expressed as words, but again whenever possible create a new title or text heading that doesn't begin with a number. In this case, you can use many of the same words in a title and just reorganize the words to avoid starting off with a number. So instead of using the title "Fifty-Nine Years After the Depression: How Much Will Seniors Remember?" you can use the title "How Much Will Seniors Remember 59 Years After the Depression?" So, in this case you would stick to the original rule of using numerals for numbers over 10 when the number is in the title but not the first word of the title.

When reporting your results, you might need to include **fractions**. APA style requires that you use words for these numbers. These types of numbers are found in about one fourth of the papers that you read in psychology journals. Get it . . . one fourth? We actually made up that fraction for this example, and we must admit that before going on to the next exciting APA rule for numbers. We have no idea how many psychology papers include common fractions. Well, at least two thirds of the authors of this book have no idea. You may have noticed that the fractions in this paragraph are not hyphenated. That's another APA rule for numbers; hyphenate fractions only when they are used as adjectives—for example, "a three-quarter turn" (see Chapter 12 for more details on when to hyphenate).

We have one more APA rule to present that tells you when to use words for numbers. Numbers are sometimes found in **commonly used phrases**. In this case, words are used for numbers. So when writing a letter in APA style to your roommate that using your toothpaste without permission violates one of the Ten Commandments, you would indeed use the word *Ten* rather than the number *10*. Or if you bring a friend back to your room to have a private conversation, you might need to post a note on your door (of course, in APA style) that states "two's company, three's a crowd." You might be writing your younger sister on her birthday and wish her a happy "sweet sixteen!" We would love to include more examples, because these are fun to write about, but we are confident you get the point.

Using Both Numerals and Words

To jazz things up a bit, APA style includes some writing-with-numbers rules that require you to write with both numerals *and* words at the same time. This applies when you're writing **back-to-back numbers**. Huh? You might be asking yourself, "When would I write two numbers back-to-back?" In your Method section you might write about the type of scales you used to collect your data. Let's say you needed to include two different scales, both of which were 5-point Likert scales. You state that **two 5**-point Likert scales measured participants' opinions. Think about experiments that include multiple independent variables. You might find multiple interactions in that experiment. In this case, you would write in your paper that "3 four-way interactions emerged."

Notice that the sentences included two different numbers back-to-back (side-by-side) and that one number is written as a word and the other number is written as a numeral. We need to tell you about one **exception** to the back-to-back numbers rule. If writing with both words and numerals makes it more difficult to understand what you're trying to get across to readers, then by all means use words in both cases. So instead of writing "The first 10 questions on the exam were not used when calculating a grade," you would write "The first ten questions . . . ." Also, if you're using ordinal numbers, then you should use only words.

> **Incorrect:** The study of social interaction included twelve four-person groups discussing stress speaking only in Pig Latin.

> **Correct:** The study of social interaction included 12 four-person groups discussing stress speaking only in Pig Latin.

> **Exception:** The first four-person group talked about stress only in Pig Latin.

How to Use Decimal Points

When to Include a Zero Before the Decimal Point

One question students often ask is when to include a zero before the decimal point when writing numbers using numerals. We are excited that we have an easy-to-follow APA rule for that question. You use a zero before the decimal point when the statistic reported is less than 1 but it **CAN** exceed 1. For example, if you're measuring the distance between the index finger and the middle finger and the measurement is 0.83 cm, you would include the zero because that measurement can exceed one. In your results section, you'll likely be asked to use Cohen's d to measure effect size (see Chapter 9); this would be reported as Cohen's $d = 0.54$ because the number can exceed 1. However, if the number cannot exceed 1, then no zero is used before the decimal fraction. You'll come across these numbers often in your results section when writing your alpha level (e.g., $p = .028$). This is also true for correlation coefficients that are always between −1 and +1, inclusive—for example, $r(59) = .63, p < .05$.

How Many Numbers Should Be Written After the Decimal Point?

This question really answers the question often heard around the world, "How should I round my numbers?" The answer: Round your answers to two decimal places as often as possible to make statistics easier to understand. Sometimes this means changing the scale (e.g., 41234 millimeters = 41.23 meters). By changing the scale, you make reading the number easier but still provide precise information. You should be able to report most data using two decimal places and still maintain precision. So when reporting your r, t, F, and X^2, you would use only two decimal places.

But wait . . . an exception to that rule! When reporting p values, report the exact p value using two **or** three decimal places. Any p values less than .001 should be written as $p < .001$. For those of you who remember older APA rules, this is a change. We used to write p values out to two decimal places (e.g., $p < .05$). This is no longer the case with most statistical calculations conducted using statistical software, unlike in the olden days when statistics were calculated by hand and tables of critical values were used to determine statistical significance.

Additional Rules for Including Numbers in Your Paper

Numbers are sometimes expressed as **Roman numerals**. If that is the common way to express those numbers, use the Roman numbers (e.g., Type I error); if not, do not use Roman numerals (e.g., Table 1, *not* Table I).

When expressing numbers, **use commas** in figures of 1,000 or more. Once again, it sounds simple, if only . . . This rule does not apply to the following: (a) page numbers (e.g., p. 3084); (b) binary digits (e.g., 0010001110); (c) serial numbers (e.g., 37194058); (d) degrees of temperature (e.g., 4013 °F); (e) acoustic frequency designations (e.g., 1000 Hz); and (f) degrees of freedom $F(1, 2900)$.

At times, you might need to include **plurals of numbers**. Many writers have an urge to include an apostrophe when using plural even thought this is not correct in any style of writing. Instead of that apostrophe, just add an s or es (e.g., 1990s, fives and sixes, 30s).

Metrication

You will sometimes need to express numbers in terms of **physical measurements** in your paper. For example, if you are studying spatial learning and memory in rats using a sand maze, you will want to include a detailed description of the maze so that others can replicate using the same apparatus. In doing so, you will need to include the physical measurements. APA style requires that all these measurements be expressed in metric units rather than in standard units. When discussing the policy on metrication, the *PM* states that metric units should be used if possible. Yes, you read it correctly . . . **if possible**. However, that section also states that if you include measurements using nonmetric units, you need to include metric equivalents *immediately* after in parentheses. For example, "To study pain perception in children, a total of 3 gal (11.36 L) of water was poured over the ice for the cold pressor task." So in other words, it is *always* possible to express your physical measurements in metric units. So much for the flexibility. To find conversions of standard measurement to metric measurement we suggest you check out http://www.sciencemadesimple.net/conversions.html. At this site, you'll also find how to express these units of measurement in full names and abbreviations. This brings us to the next APA rule.

When Do You Use Abbreviations?

When you **write your measurements** using metric units, you can use the **abbreviation** for the unit of measurement after the numeral, and remember that these abbreviations do not include a period unless they are found at the end of a sentence (e.g., 5 cm). Abbreviations are expressed in **lowercase letters,** though there are exceptions to this rule because you want to avoid confusion of the abbreviation for liter, "L," being misread as the number one. When you use a symbol, you need to insert a space between the symbol and the number it refers to (e.g., 10 m). Warning! There is an exception to this spacing rule. When you write about measures of angles in degrees, minutes, and seconds, no space is required (e.g., 60° angle, 10,' 5").

When circumstances call for you to describe what metric unit you used for your measurement, you no longer use abbreviations. In those situations, you should **write out the measurement term;** the term should not follow a numeric value (e.g., "Distance was measured in centimeters"). Notice that you use **lowercase letters** to write out the names of units. The typical exceptions apply here (e.g., used in a title, beginning of a sentence). And our favorite type of APA rule, an exception to an exception is next. Lowercase letters are still used in titles when you include a symbol rather than the full name of the metric unit. Honestly, we think the better idea is to not use the symbol but to instead just spell it out. Including a symbol in your title is awkward to begin with.

You might also need to express these **units of measurement** in plural form (e.g., centimeters). Did we just include an example to illustrate a plural form of a measurement? We apologize for that. APA style requires that when writing out the full name of the measurement, you express the term in plural (e.g., "length was measured in centimeters"). Yes, we just gave that same example again. However, when you use the abbreviation for a metric unit, even when there is more than one of that unit, it is *not* expressed in plural units. This means stating that you used "50 cm" and not "50 cms."

To summarize, we have just one thing to say. If you are shocked by the number of rules that apply to expressing numbers in an APA-style paper, you are not alone. Most people feel the same way, and we sure did when we first ran into them. But we all know the rules and can be stronger writers in APA style because of it.

Table 11.1 Expressing Numbers in APA Format

Type of Number	How to Express	Example
10 and up	Numbers	300 apples
Less than 10	Words	Three apples
Numbers in an abstract	Numbers	3 students
Mathematics	Numbers	Divided by 3
Numbers with a measurement	Numbers	3.57 cm
Numbers in a graph	Numbers	$M = 86$
Numbered series	Numbers	Column 4
Time, dates, ages, scores, points on a scale, exact sums of money, numbers as numbers	Numbers	$4.17; 1 hr 20 min February 12, 2009, at 2:20 p.m. 4 years old 3 on a 5-point scale the number 7
Approximation for days, months, and years	Words	We landed on the moon approximately forty years ago.
Numbers beginning a title or heading	Words	Fourteen Hundred and Ninety-Two: A Year to Remember
Numbers beginning a sentence	Words	Seventy percent of the sample
Common fractions	Words	one third of participants
Universally accepted usage	Words	Thirty Years War
Lists of numbers	Numerals if list includes four or more numbers; words if list includes three or fewer numbers	Subjects could choose among 1, 2, 3, 4, or 5 pathways. Subjects could choose among one, two, or three pathways.

Table 11.2 Exceptions to the Number Rules

Type of Rule	Exception	Example
Expressing numbers 10 and up	Combine words and numbers for back-to-back numbers	Twelve 3-year-olds
Report statistics to two decimal places	Report to two or three decimal places for p	$p < .001$ or $p = .036$
Abbreviations expressed in lowercase letters	Uppercase letters for liters, ambiguous abbreviations	7 L for liters
Space between the symbol and the number it refers to	Measures of angles in degrees, minutes, seconds . . . no space	45°, 11', 2"
Commas in figures of 1,000 or more	Page numbers Binary digits Serial numbers Degrees of temperature Acoustic frequency designations Degrees of freedom	p. 3084 0010001110 37194058 4013 °F 1000 Hz $F(1, 2900)$
Capitalize words in a title	Abbreviations for measurement	*An Examination of 35 mm of the Brain*

Formatting 12

*Organizing, Headings, and Making
Your Work Look Good to Print*

A fter your hard work creating the scientific story for your paper by reading the literature, writing your paper, creating logical arguments in your Introduction to support your hypothesis with findings from the literature, and developing methodology to test your hypothesis, it is time to take a different focus and examine the formatting of your paper. As you read in Chapter 1, APA format is what makes a journal article consistent with scientific norms. This may sound trivial, but you are probably not surprised that the APA *PM* provides answers to almost all your formatting questions. And keep in mind, the ability to follow instructions and attention to detail are important skills that employers value highly. Following these instructions will create a paper that makes a good impression even before one starts to read it. Although the quality of your writing is of utmost importance together with the rigor of your research, even these small details can make a difference when deciding between an A and an A–. So read on to learn the order of the parts of the manuscript, the headings you should use, the size of your margins, and when and when not to indent. In Chapter 14, we provide instructions for how to use Word to format the different sections of your APA paper. In Chapter 19 you will find a sample paper that provides an illustration of exactly what your paper should look like before you turn it in.

What Goes Where?

Let's start with ordering the parts of your manuscript. Just use the following order for the different sections of your paper, and you're already on the right track. We've also noted when you need to start a section on a new page.

Title page

Abstract (new page)

Introduction (new page; the word "Introduction" not needed)

Method

Results

Discussion

References (new page)

Table/s (new page)

Figure/s (new page)

Appendix (new page)

A common mistake we see our students make is to start a new page for the different sections in the main text of their papers. For example, many students often feel compelled to start their Method section on a "fresh" page just after the Introduction. We think it is somewhat of an automatic behavior—the need to separate the big sections of the text physically. As we tell our students, "When in doubt, double-space throughout!" We've also seen our students thinking "green," and in an attempt to conserve paper, they type some sections that *do* require new pages (e.g., References) directly after the preceding section. As long as we're on the topic, APA style does not allow you to print your paper on both sides of the page. You can check with your instructor to see if double-siding is permissible; we understand the waste of using only one side of each page. We will say that it is easier to edit/grade a paper printed on one side compared with one printed on both sides.

What Your Paper Should Look Like

Fonts, Margins, and Indents

Let's start with the rules that influence how your paper looks. When you start writing your paper, you need to pick a **font** and **font size** that is easy to read. APA recommends Times New Roman in 12-point size. This is not a place to flaunt your individuality. Set your default to this font. The one place you can use a different font is your figures, with APA recommending sans serif type (e.g., Arial, Helvetica, Tahoma, Verdana). Check out Chapter 14 for details on how to change fonts in Word and Chapter 19 with the sample paper to see an example of these different fonts. Really you just want to avoid the fonts that make it difficult to read your paper. Honestly, your best bet is to stick to *Times New Roman*. Leave the calligraphy to those greeting cards and fancy invitations. Whatever font you choose, use the default spacing between letters and words, but be careful not to use the default spacing between paragraphs. Sometimes in Word 2007, the default spacing is 1.15 (we know . . . an odd choice), when it should be 2.0—double-spaced.

Next, we need to cover setting your **margins**. We know this is an issue when you have a particular page length you want to achieve and you've played with your paper margins in the past to get your paper to be the correct number of pages. We need to break the news . . . APA requires 1-inch margins throughout. That means the top and bottom margins, as well as the margins to the left and right, are all uniform (see Chapter 14 for instructions on how to set margins). For your instructors who do not yet use Word to track changes to provide feedback, those margins provide enough room for them to give you all the information you need to improve your paper or a place to write their rave reviews. Be sure to justify the margins only on the left. This means all lines on the left of the page will be even, and the lines on the right of your paper will be uneven. See Chapter 14 for details on how to correctly justify the left margin and maintain a ragged right margin using Word. Within these margins is where you get to read all the red ink that some instructors love to use when marking sections that need to be reviewed. Do not take all that red ink personally. Two ideas to share here: (a) Red ink or any color of ink on your paper in general means that your instructor cares enough to give you detailed feedback to help improve your writing, and (b) every writer's writing can be improved; your authors marked up one another's chapters continuously throughout the creation of this book. Remember, the ultimate goal is to communicate as clearly as you can. If you remember that goal, you may come to appreciate the red ink. But honestly, the red ink is just a color that can be easily seen as different from the black ink on your paper.

When writing your paper, be sure to **indent** the first line of each paragraph using the typical five- to seven-space indent; normally just using the "tab" key will do. APA style does have a few exceptions for indenting. You *do not* indent for the following parts of your paper: (a) the first line of the abstract paragraph, (b) block quotations, (c) titles or heading Levels 1 and 2, (d) table titles, and (e) figure captions. Sometimes, the software you use will automatically make this indent the right size, around five to seven spaces. You'll remember from Chapter 10 that you use hanging indents for the reference list, which means that for each separate reference item, all lines except the first line are indented five to seven spaces. Again, the "hanging" part of that term refers to the first line hanging to the left of the rest of the lines. Skip ahead to Chapter 14 for the how-to on formatting with hanging indents.

Running Head

Although the text of your paper needs to have 1-inch margins, you need to place your running head within that 1 inch space at the top of the page; place the page header information at 0.5 inches. The words "Running head" appear on only page 1 of your paper (see Chapter 14 for the Word instructions on how to do this). Including a running head is important given the possibility that your professor could throw your paper and those of other students into the air (it's possible), resulting in a confetti of pages. Once the excitement passes, the realization sets in that these papers need to be placed back in the correct order with the correct pages going with the right paper. That is where the information in your running head comes into play. Each page of your paper includes in the upper left corner an abbreviated title (a short description) of your paper and the page number in the upper right corner (see the sample paper in Chapter 19). Your abbreviated title needs to be 50 characters or less (including all spaces and punctuation) and in all uppercase letters, placed flush with the left margin. This is what will allow all pages of your paper to be identified as part of your paper. Typically, this shorter title is your longer title with fewer words. For example:

Title: Effects of Type of Lineup on the Accuracy of Children's Person Identification

Abbreviated Title: ACCURACY OF CHILDREN'S PERSON IDENTIFICATION

On your title page, you include the words "Running head" followed by a colon before your abbreviated title. For all pages that follow, include only your abbreviated title. All pages of your paper are numbered (also called paginated), including your tables and figures, starting with the first page. Place the page number in the running head you create, flush with the right margin. If you use the *Header* function under the *Insert* tab in Word 2007 (see *Header* and *Footer* under the *View* menu in Word 2003) you won't need to type this information separately on each page. Instead, you can type it in the Header space one time, create a different first page (by clicking on *Different First Page* in the *Design* tab in Word 2007; see Chapter 14 for instructions) so that you can include the words "Running head," and you are good to go for the whole paper.

Headings

To help organize an APA-style paper, five different levels of headings are used. There are rules about when to use these different headings. You'll see that choosing the headings depends on the section of your paper and the number of experiments you are writing about. We've included a list of these headings in the table that follows; a separate table tells you when to use each of the headings.

Level	How to Format
1	**Centered, Boldface, First Letter of Important Words Capitalized**
2	**Flush Left, Boldface, First Letter of Important Words Capitalized**
3	**Indented, boldface, first letter of first word capitalized, end with a period.**
4	***Indented, boldface, italicized, first letter of first word capitalized, end with a period.***
5	*Indented, italicized, first letter of first word capitalized, end with a period.*

In case you're wondering what makes a word "important" enough to be capitalized in headings and titles, here are a couple of things to remember: (a) Capitalize *any* word of four or more letters (e.g., *with, from, into*), and (b) capitalize all verbs (e.g., *are, be, can, is, was*), nouns (e.g., *end, gun, ink, net*), pronouns (e.g., *it, he, she, him, her*), adverbs (e.g., *far, if, not, too*), and adjectives (e.g., *big, few, low, new*). Here are some words that should *not* be capitalized in headings and titles: conjunctions (e.g., *and, but, or*), articles (e.g., *a, an, the*), and prepositions less than four letters long (e.g., *in, at, to, off, for*).

There are two **exceptions** to the Level 1 heading rules. You *do not* use boldface for your abstract or reference section heading. Why? Good question. We dug around for an answer but came up empty. If we were in charge of APA style, we would have made all headings boldface. Not using boldface for the abstract and reference sections just seems like an easy way to confuse everyone. But obviously we are not the ones writing the rules—just trying to make them easier to understand. When typing the paragraph that follows heading Levels 1 and 2, start the paragraph on a new line. For Levels 3, 4, and 5, start the paragraph on the same line as the heading. Always remember to continue to double-space your paper when using the different levels of headings. Next, we'll go over when you use each of these headings.

If you are writing a one-experiment paper:	
Level	When to Use
1	For each of the main sections of your paper (e.g., Method, Results, Discussion)
2	For the subsections of the Method section (e.g., Participants, Procedure)
3	For the subsections of subsections of the Method section (e.g., Surveys, Software)

Typically, you will use only two headings levels in your paper. In Chapter 19, you'll see a sample paper written with two headings levels. Take a quick look to understand how these headings appear within a paper.

If you have multiple experiments in your paper:	
Level	When to Use
1	For the start of each separate study (e.g., Experiment 1)
2	For each of the main sections of each study (e.g., Method, Results, Discussion)
3	For the subsections of the Method section (e.g., Participants, Procedure)

One common mistake we see when students are first learning APA style is that they use the word *Introduction* as a heading rather than simply retyping their title above the introduction of the paper. For that heading, you use Level 1 whether you have a single or multiple experiments.

Spelling Matters: Spelling Rules and Capitalization

We have all gotten used to the wonderful spell-checker provided by Word. We believe that Bill Gates usually provides the correct spelling for us. However, sometimes Bill is wrong and we need additional guidance—or Bill does not have an extensive knowledge of our discipline and its jargon. Additional spelling guidance should come from *Merriam-Webster's Collegiate Dictionary* (2005), where word spelling conforms to standard American English spelling. At times, the word you are looking up (and we always love looking up words we can't spell) might not be in *Webster's Collegiate,* in which case you'll need to look in *Webster's Third New International Dictionary* (2002). Yes, you will need to be a global speller! Finally, when it comes to psychological terms, you can also refer to the *APA Dictionary of Psychology* (VandenBos, 2007). In some cases, you'll find that a word has multiple spelling options. For word spelling, always use the first spelling provided in these sources (e.g., use *color* rather than *colour* and *toward* instead of *towards*).

Plural Words

Sometimes just adding an *s* or an *es* to a word is not the way to go when making a singular word a plural word. This is particularly true for the plural forms of **words of Latin or Greek** origin. Given that we spend a great deal of time collecting data, this is one word to be familiar with when it comes to the plural form. One of the most common mistakes is the word *data*. This is the plural word for the singular *datum*. We rarely talk about the datum from our research because we typically collect findings from multiple participants or multiple times. Therefore you'll use the word *data*. Just remember that this word is plural, and therefore the verb that follows should also be plural. So this is an example when the *um* becomes an *a* when the word is made plural. Another example: Sometimes an *x* becomes *ces* (e.g., *appendix, appendices*). For other words of this origin, the singular *non* becomes *na* (e.g., *phenomenon, phenomena*).

Plurals are often needed when using the possessive form of a group of individuals. The common question asked in this case is whether to add the **apostrophe before the *s* or after the *s*.** The easiest way to make a singular name possessive is to add an apostrophe and an *s* (e.g., Little Albert's). But when forming the possessive of a plural name, add an *s* before an apostrophe (e.g., the Pavlovs'). An **exception:** If the singular noun ends in an unpronounced *s*, you use only an apostrophe after that *s* (e.g., Descartes'). No need for another *s*.

Keep in mind when you do pronounce the *s* of a name you add an *es* before the apostrophe (e.g., the Ebbinghauses').

Finally, the other issue with regard to plurals concerns the confusion about when to just use an *s* or an *es* to indicate the plural form for a name. The rules are very simple: To indicate the name of the group of people whose name ends in *s,* add *es* (e.g., the Calkinses). If the name does not end in an *s* then you add an *s* (e.g., the Horneys). OK, clearly a table will help out here, so see Table 12.1 for more examples of the rules for singular and plural spelling of words.

Table 12.1 Examples of Some Singular and Plural Words Demonstrating Key Rules

Singular	Plural
Datum	Data
Stigma	Stigmata
Wells	Wellses
Lanning	Lannings
Smith's (possessive)	Smiths' (possessive)
Doe's (possessive)	Does' (possessive)

Hyphenation

When should you use a hyphen? This question is raised when dealing with compound words, which can be written in a number of different ways. Although not something we think of often, the use of a hyphen can dramatically change the meaning of a sentence. When you write about a dirty-movie theater you are addressing a different issue than when you write about a dirty movie theater. In the first case you are discussing the type of movie, and in the second case you are addressing the cleanliness of the theater itself. So you see, a little hyphen can make all the difference in the world. Therefore, correctly using the hyphen can make your writing more clearly express your intended meaning. Often, the use of a hyphen for a compound word will be determined by the context of the sentence. For some compound words, the words can be spelled both with and without a hyphen. In those cases, simply use the first spelling found in the dictionary. There you will find whether to use the compound words as a single word (e.g., *overachiever*), with a hyphen (e.g., *over-the-counter*), or finally as two separate words (e.g., *work group*). In other cases, you need to follow the APA principles for hyphens. Tables 12.2 and 12.3 differentiate when and when not to use a hyphen. In both tables, you find a list of the rules followed by examples to illustrate the rules.

Table 12.2 When to Hyphenate	
The Rule	**An Example of the Rule**
Hyphenate . . .	
To make sure compound adjectives are not misread	Iced-tea cup (vs. cup of iced tea); thrill-seeking teenagers
To help the reader understand the intended meaning of two or more adjectives before a noun that act as one idea	First-class seat; top-notch idea
When the combination of an adjective and a noun precedes the noun	Same-sex marriage

When prefixes are followed by
   capitalized words
   numbers
   abbreviations
   more than one word
	
	neo-Freudian
	post-911 years
	non-APA members
	post-20th-century invention

When using the prefix *self*	Self-report; self-confident
When the prefix can create a word with a different meaning	Re-cover the sofa; re-lease the apartment
When using two or more compound words with a common base used only once in the sentence	2-, 3-, and 4-year-olds
To avoid doubling a vowel	De-emphasize
Using cardinal numbers	Twenty-seven
Using fractions as adjectives	One-third minority

Table 12.3 When Not to Hyphenate	
The Rule	**An Example of the Rule**
Don't hyphenate . . .	
A compound with *ly*	Happily married couples
A compound with a comparative or superlative	Higher optimism scores
Chemical terms	Sodium glutamate compound

(Continued)

Table 12.3 (Continued)

The Rule	An Example of the Rule
A modifier using a phrase from a foreign language	a priori argument
Describing phrase that uses a numeral or letter in the second part	Type I error
Fractions as nouns	Three fourths of the students
When using most prefixes	Pretest

Capitalization

Compared with whether to include a hyphen, you'll likely find that an easier decision is whether to use an upper- or lowercase letter. But . . . think again. APA has so many rules related to when to capitalize that we decided it was best to list the many times when you should capitalize the first letter of a word. You'll find the different rules listed in Table 12.4. Though some of the APA format rules

Table 12.4 When to Capitalize

The Rule	An Example of the Rule
The first word of a sentence	You should capitalize the first word of a sentence.
The first word following a colon	Two basic instances in which you capitalize: The first word of a sentence is capitalized, and the first word of a complete thought following a colon is capitalized.
All words of four letters or more in titles of books or articles when they appear within a paper	In his book *Undergraduate Writing in Psychology: Learning to Tell the Scientific Story* (2008), Landrum presents students with a step-by-step guide for scientific writing.
The first word of titles of books and journal articles in your reference lists; all major words of a journal title	Wilson, J. H., Stadler, J. R., Schwartz, B. M., & Goff, D. M. (2009). Touching your students: The impact of a handshake on the first day of class. *Journal of the Scholarship of Teaching and Learning*.
When you reference a section of the paper you are writing	As you see in the Method section, all participants were less than 6 years old.

The Rule	An Example of the Rule
Proper names	Margaret Floy Washburn
Specific department name at a specific university or college; specific course offered	The Department of Psychology at Randolph College offers Health Psychology as an upper-level lab course.
Brand names of drugs, food, equipment	Paxil, Cheezits, Kleenex
Nouns followed by numerals	In Experiment 4; as shown in Table 3; as illustrated in Chapter 10
Exact titles of tests/assessments	Peabody Picture Vocabulary Test; Beck Depression Inventory
Names of conditions or groups in your experiment (when the name of the condition follows)	Condition A; Condition 2
Variable names with multiplication signs	Suggestibility × Age × Sex

will seem obvious and follow what you would expect when typing a paper, you'll see there are a few instances that are specific to APA format.

We see the most capitalization errors when our students are preparing their References section. For book titles and journal article titles, you capitalize (a) the first word, (b) the first word after a colon, and (c) proper nouns (see Chapter 4 for a review of what constitutes a proper noun).

Final Touches

We have a few final words of advice before you hand in your paper. Take a close look at Chapter 18 that provides you with some how-tos on proofreading and Chapter 17, which will review how to use a rubric to make sure you have covered all the guidelines provided by your instructor. We can assure you that both steps can significantly improve your writing and your grade. In addition to your instructor's rubric, we have also provided a checklist for you on the back flap of the book. The checklist will help you make sure you have avoided the most common errors we come across in student papers and some of the APA style and format rules you'll want to double-check before handing in your masterpiece.

Table That Motion 13

The Special Challenges of Tables and Figures

Did you use some interesting visual stimuli in your research study? Do you have so many numbers (e.g., means and standard deviations) from your statistical analyses that writing them out in the text of your paper would be cumbersome? If the answer to either of these questions is yes, these are just two of the reasons that you may have to use tables or figures in your paper. Some undergraduate papers that are not associated with reporting research do not need either figures or tables. That said, we know that some instructors and professors require a Table 1 in papers for their research methods classes, precisely to practice formatting a table. Papers assigned for experimental or research design classes typically do require some display of results, and such assignments are often designed explicitly to give you training in table and figure design. You may be surprised to note that even literature reviews can sometimes use a table and even a figure.

What's What

A well-designed table can actually save space compared with repetitive paragraphs presenting boatloads (a technical term) of numbers. A figure can help tell a story that words in text cannot communicate as well; perhaps a picture can be worth a thousand words at times. Tables and figures can be extremely effective writing tools when used appropriately—which is what this chapter is all about.

Tables are most often rows and columns of descriptive data (e.g., means, standard deviations), the results of inferential analyses (e.g., correlations or other analyses), or sometimes even words (e.g., sample items from a scale or questionnaire). Figures are essentially everything else: line graphs, pie charts, histograms, bar charts, photographs of stimuli material, or even flowcharts to illustrate key variables and hypotheses. Often, a bar graph or even a pie chart can illustrate your data in a clearer way than could writing it out as text in your Results section. In fact, when you are presenting a poster for a conference, it is preferable to use a figure to illustrate your data because your findings are typically more quickly absorbed if done right and space is not a problem. Space? Yes, one of the reasons researchers are often urged not to use figures and sometimes even to avoid tables is that tables and figures take up more space on the printed page where, for journals, every page costs money to produce. This is not something one has to worry about when turning in a paper for a class assignment. The primary consideration is this: Does a *table or figure describe your results more clearly?*

Although adding figures and tables provides a nice visual to your paper, use them in a paper only if they are going to help the reader better understand your results and what you did. For example, it is clearly easier to create a table describing the results of correlations than listing each and every correlational coefficient, sample size, and p value in your text. If you are listing means and you have fewer than four means to list, do not use a table; instead, describe the means in your results section (APA, 2010a). In fact, a cursory scan of journal articles over the years shows that what was often presented in a table in older journal articles is now presented directly in the text. A good example is the reporting of results of statistical significance tests (e.g., reporting whether many different t tests or an analysis of variance [ANOVA] was significant). If you are testing the relation between variables (e.g., is amount of sleep one gets correlated with how many pages of notes that person takes in class?) or whether two or more groups are different from each other (e.g., did the group of students who drank two cans of an energy drink pay more attention to the lecture than the group of students who did not?), you need statistical tests to establish whether findings are at chance levels or beyond chance levels. If the results are beyond chance levels, then we start to think about whether the independent variables can explain the results (see Chapter 9).

A simple way to check whether you need a table or figure is to see if you can describe what you want to put into a table or figure clearly and simply in your text. Of course, another consideration is if you have been explicitly required to include a table or figure as part of your assignment. Bottom line: The main goal of tables and figures is to help you present a lot of information efficiently and to make those data easier to understand (APA, 2010a). If you can achieve these two goals without tables and figures, avoid them (and more power to you). By the way, this is a good time to also look at our chapter on Results sections (see Chapter 9).

Getting the Look Down

Like many other key elements of an APA-style paper, such as in-text citations, it is easy for a reader to see if you have used correct APA style for your table or figure. Even more important, make sure you know how to use your word processing program to set up your tables correctly using tabs and indents where needed.

In other words, do not just use your space bar and Enter key to replicate the look of our sample table or a journal article table. It is also a good idea to avoid using the tables provided by statistical programs such as SPSS (Statistical Package for the Social Sciences) or Excel, as these programmed options are often not exactly APA-style compliant and tweaking them will probably take more work than creating the table from scratch. The next chapter (Chapter 14) shows you how to create APA-style tables in Word.

Let's start with tables. Take a look at the sample table in Table 13.1 (adapted from Gurung & Johnson, 2010). Table 13.1 shows you a basic way of reporting correlations and also includes descriptive data. Note that the numbering of tables for chapters in a book is different than for papers or articles; you will not see decimal points in table numbers in articles. And yes, we really needed a table here to illustrate the format for an APA-style table. Another note: We are following our convention of using a different font to show examples of what *you* would do when writing your paper; however, just remember that this table would be in a Times New Roman 12-point font in *your* paper.

Table 13.1 Mean Values, Standard Deviations, and Intercorrelations of Control Variables

Measure	*M*	*SD*	1	2	3	4	5
1. Objectification	4.07	11.03	—				
2. Self-objectification	3.92	12.37	.64***	—			
3. Self-esteem	4.54	.82	.24**	.29***	—		
4. Benevolent sexism	3.21	.87	−.15	−.02	−.06	—	
5. Hostile sexism	3.26	.91	−.11	−.01	−.07	.50***	—

$*p < .05.$ $**p < .01.$ $***p < .001.$

Every table has a number identified at the top of the page (e.g., Table X, where *X* is the number of the table). The table title is next, typed in *italics,* with the first letter of each major word (i.e., not *of, the, and*) capitalized. Your titles should provide the reader with a clear sense of what the table holds.

Incorrect: *Descriptive Data*

Correct: *Mean Values, Standard Deviations, and Intercorrelations of Control Variables*

Each column of data should have a clear heading that is not too long. Sometimes two columns, and correspondingly two headings, may need an additional and higher level heading that describes both columns (e.g., see Table 13.2). Some common abbreviations such as *M* for mean or *SD* for standard deviation can be used without your having to define them in the note section, but note that statistical symbols and notations, including *M* and *SD,* should be italicized in the table. There is one exception: If those items appear in the italicized table title, then "un-italicize" them; the whole point is to bring attention to the statistical notation.

The title is followed by an underline (or "rule") ("___") that runs horizontally across the top of the table. There are several ways to create this line: Press the shift key and the key between the 0 and = keys (do not use the underline function of your word processor) and hold them down until your line is the desired length, or you can insert a line by hitting that same key—the hyphen key—three times at the beginning of the line and then hitting Enter. Cool trick, eh? These underlines appear under the title and headings, as major dividers in the table itself, and at the bottom of the table above the Note. There is no line under the Note. Feel free to use white space instead of a line to separate sections or blocks of data. You can also use some of the tips presented in Chapter 14 to use Word to create a table, but no matter which method you use, be sure to follow the rules of APA format for tables.

In Table 13.1, notice that the numbers line up below the decimal point. Remember to report your results in tables using two or three decimal places. If you are reporting correlations, you do not need to use a zero in front of the decimal point because correlations cannot exceed 1 and no zero is needed for any statistic that cannot be greater than 1 (see Chapter 11). **Important error to avoid:** Probability values to your table Notes should use $p < .01$, $p < .05$, and $p < .001$ (with periods between each p value), even though your results section should use exact probability values (as discussed in Chapter 9). Speaking of numbers, report correlations of a variable with itself as a dash ("—"), as seen in Table 13.1. This dash is called an "em dash" (it's the length of an *m* in whatever typeface you're using); press Ctrl + Alt + the minus sign on the number keypad to make one.

Table 13.2 shows you a basic table representing means for an experiment with three conditions. With the data for all three conditions in one table, the reader can easily compare the means across conditions. It also saves text space, and it represents a clear case for when a table can save a lot of space. Of note is that when Valerie Johnson (from whose paper the table is taken) first created the table, she had a separate table for each category of variables (e.g., Objectification, Competence). Although it did seem to be less cluttered than what you see in Table 13.2, it precluded a reader's comparing means across category *and* condition. Always combine tables when you can. If you have a really long table and it will not fit on one page (Table 13.2 did not fit on one page when this chapter was first written in Word and not typeset on the printed page), you need to repeat the title on each page. After the first page, add the word *continued* surrounded by parentheses "( )" at the end.

The tables you see here represent the most common tables needed for students learning to write their first papers in APA format. As the complexity of the research design increases, the table complexity and formatting complexity increase as well. Some tables will need divider lines or spaces between blocks

Table 13.2 Mean Values of the Control Variables and Dependent Variables Separated by Condition

Variable	Control[a]		Athletic		Academic	
	M	**SD**	**M**	**SD**	**M**	**SD**
Competence						
Competent***	5.81	1.23	6.90	1.17	6.42	1.44
Determined***	5.99	1.31	7.84	0.96	6.71	1.45
Independent***	5.58	1.54	6.99	1.18	6.22	1.56
Intelligent***	5.66	1.08	6.87	1.19	6.92	1.64
Responsible***	5.51	1.41	7.10	1.21	6.15	1.62
Studious***	5.33	1.42	6.60	1.28	6.68	1.73
Talented***	6.08	1.08	7.93	0.98	6.55	1.37
Objectification						
Attractive	6.74	1.12	6.78	1.31	6.49	1.52
Desirable***	6.33	1.39	6.72	1.22	6.10	1.50
Promiscuous***	6.12	1.65	4.71	1.54	5.59	2.13
Sexy*	6.42	1.59	6.41	1.40	6.03	1.65
Short-term fling***	6.61	1.70	4.62	1.66	5.70	2.21
Uses body***	6.26	1.80	4.80	1.84	5.65	2.25
Personal characteristics						
Feminine***	7.85	1.07	7.13	1.36	7.38	1.23
Fit/healthy***	7.27	1.22	8.20	1.63	6.32	1.63
High self-esteem***	6.95	1.36	7.17	1.25	6.39	1.63
Honest***	5.57	1.27	6.32	1.21	5.84	1.46
Shallow***	5.12	1.77	4.12	1.47	4.74	1.84
Vain***	5.51	1.79	4.77	1.54	5.30	1.79
Fillers						
Appropriateness***	5.36	1.77	6.63	1.66	4.82	2.29
Likeable***	6.47	1.22	6.78	1.19	6.14	1.28
Popular***	7.07	1.19	7.01	1.25	6.32	1.52
Revealingness***	5.24	1.86	4.10	2.10	5.33	2.32
Trustworthy***	5.49	1.21	6.47	1.24	5.87	1.58

Note. Table used with permission from Valerie Johnson, University of Wisconsin–Green Bay.

[a]Models in the control condition wore the same outfits as those in the two experimental conditions.

*$p < .05$. ***$p < .001$.

of numbers. Remember, there are never vertical lines in an APA-formatted table; only horizontal lines when needed.

A Note on "Notes"

If a table has a note, that note is placed at the very bottom of the table, and the word *Note* or *Notes* is italicized. There is an order to what goes into this section. First, and right after the period (use a period, not a colon or semicolon), you list definitions of abbreviations, if any, and "general" information that pertains to the entire table. General notes may include the source of your information. On a separate line, list a "probability note," which explains what the asterisks in the table mean. Sometimes you may need to use a "specific" note (between the general and probability notes on its own line) if you have information that relates only to specific columns or rows. For example, you may want to indicate that the means in a certain column or for a certain variable were different. You do so using a superscript lowercase letter (e.g., [a, b, c]). See Table 13.2 for examples of each of these notes.

Figuring It Out

It is rare to need a figure for most papers written for undergraduate classes because the data represented in most figures can be more easily and effectively written in the body of the paper. Figures are particularly helpful for illustrating the results of complex statistical analyses and intricate research designs. Neither of those situations is common when you are first learning to do research and write in APA style. However, your design could easily include two variables. In that case, a figure might be best to illustrate a finding that includes an interaction of those variables. An additional possible use of figures is when you use photographic stimuli and a description will not suffice or when you have a really complex research design and want to use a chart to illustrate the research design. Mind you, these exceptions can be common. The tables used as examples (Tables 13.1 and 13.2) refer to a study in which participants saw photographs of students provocatively attired and in different contexts (e.g., a swimming pool, in a classroom, against a blank wall). The researchers measured the extent to which the student models were objectified (Johnson & Gurung, 2010). Describing the clothing and contexts—the main experimental stimuli and variants—does not provide a reader with a good idea of the experiment. This is one place where it may be necessary to include photographs (and the authors did do so in their paper). Although using photographs may imply brightening up your paper with color, use only black-and-white versions of photographs and even for all other figures. Some journals allow color figures, although most do not. Ask your instructor what he or she prefers in this regard.

Figures are also very useful for depicting the relations between different variables. Figure 13.1 illustrates how the complex relationship between

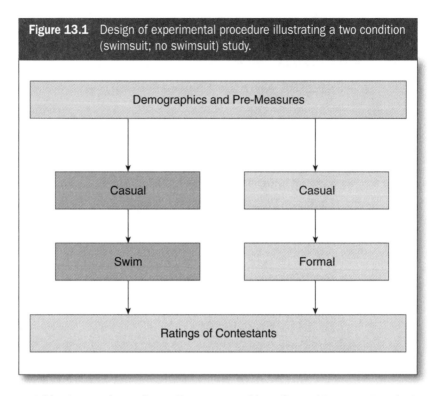

Figure 13.1 Design of experimental procedure illustrating a two condition (swimsuit; no swimsuit) study.

variables in a study can be easily represented by a figure (Gurung, Morack, & Bloch, 2005). Note that the figure has a "caption," which also serves as a title ("Design of experimental procedure illustrating a two condition (swimsuit; no swimsuit) study.") Figures do not include a separate title.

Get *Legendary* (and Use Captions)

Tables have titles; figures have "captions." Also in contrast to tables, the caption is placed below the figure (as shown in Figure 13.1) and in many ways combines the title and notes sections of tables. A caption always starts with the word *Figure* in italics and has the number of the figure followed by a period (e.g., *Figure X.*). Again use whole numbers similar to how tables are numbered. Follow the number with a clear but concise description of what the figure shows.

A legend is the descriptive information within a figure that identifies key components of the figure. For example, a graph with x (horizontal and always the independent variable for an experiment) and y (vertical and the dependent variable) axes should have the axes labeled. In Figure 13.2 the vertical axis represents scores on an exam. The horizontal axis represents Exams 1 and 2. The legend explains how the shaded bars represent the students who either did an extra credit assignment or not. For legends, as for table titles, capitalize only major words.

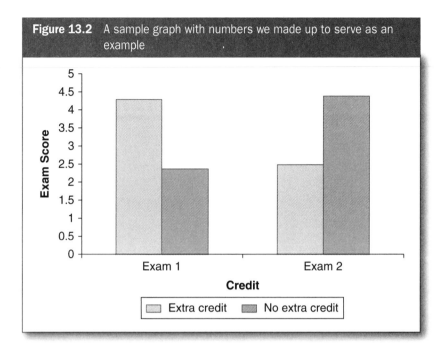

Figure 13.2 A sample graph with numbers we made up to serve as an example

Where to Place Tables and Figures

So you know you need a figure or table but wonder where to place it or them in your paper. If you were submitting a manuscript for review for publication to a journal, your tables and figures would be the last pages of your paper. Your table or tables would follow your references and footnotes (if applicable), and your figure or figures would go last. Most instructors also want your tables and figures to be similarly placed. In the published article, your tables and figures will be placed in the text. Some instructors actually like the tables and figures to be placed within your manuscript closest to where they are described (and this is what we did when we first wrote these chapters). Although this organization would be incorrect according to APA format, be sure to ask how or where your instructor would like the tables and figures placed, and then be sure to follow your instructor's guidelines. If your paper does include a figure or table, you need to include a reference to the table at the appropriate point of the paper, almost always in the Results section. You need to use only the table or figure number; do not worry about (or include) the location (i.e., *above* or *below* or on page *X* of your paper). As we described in Chapter 9, references to your tables/figures can be directly within the sentence or within parentheses as seen in the two examples that follow and should tell the reader what is presented in the table.

Incorrect: Results are presented in Table 1.

Correct: Means and correlations between the major variables appear in Table 1.

Correct: There were significant correlations between the major variables (see Table 1).

But I Am Doing a Literature Review: Could I Use a Table or Figure?

We began this chapter by suggesting that, indeed, you could use a table or figure even when doing a literature review, so the answer is yes. Mind you, the emphasis is on *could*. You rarely *have* to, but often, a table summarizing key findings or research articles/citations can come in very handy. A figure can be used to visually map out theoretical ideas or links between variables and concepts described in the paper. Figure 13.1 provides a good example.

Don't Forget

- If you revise your paper and redo some analyses and find you have to change your table, make sure to go back to your Results and/or Discussion section(s) to change related material.
- Watch your formatting. Pay close attention to the labels and positioning of labels in relation to the rest of your material.
- Avoid abbreviating material unless absolutely necessary, and if you do, make sure you explain your abbreviation in a table Note.
- Number your tables/figures in the order in which they are needed in your paper, and use only whole numbers (e.g., Table 1, Table 2—not Table 1.5 or Table 1a, Table 1b). In case you're wondering, tables are numbered in this book by chapter plus the order in which the tables appear in a chapter—Table 13.1, Table 13.2—but your paper won't have chapters, so you need only whole numbers.
- Plagiarism rules still apply (see Chapter 5). Do not copy a table or figure from another published work without getting permission (yes, tedious, but needed even if you have adapted the material) and also citing the source.
- Don't go table/figure crazy. Most 10- to 15-page papers (a guess as to the average undergraduate paper length) need not have more than one or two tables/figures. Consolidate where appropriate, while always following the teacher's instructions.
- Tables and figures should not duplicate material in the text.
- Tell your reader, in the text, exactly what is presented in the table or figure you include.

Tables and figures are pretty nice to have to break up the monotony of text and to illustrate what you did. Although you may not have a need to create one for your research paper, it may be good practice to include one if you can. There are a lot of details to pay attention to, but relevant tables and figures truly make an article much more palatable.

Make Microsoft Word 2007 Work for You

14

APA Formatting

Every job, every occupation, and every career has tools of the trade. One of the key skills you can acquire during your undergraduate career is the ability to write clearly and succinctly. One of the tools of your trade will be Microsoft Word (Word from here on). There may be times when you attempt to get by with substitutions (OpenOffice, WordPerfect), but to achieve the attention to detail that an APA-formatted paper requires, Word is your best bet (and no, we do not get royalties from Microsoft for this quasi-endorsement). In this chapter, we present some of the common tasks you'll need to master when preparing a paper in APA format; we show you the menus and guide you through the process of making all this happen. As you try to achieve any of the tasks in this chapter, you may want to lay your book flat next to your computer, with Word open, so that you can follow our instructions step-by-step.

Word 2007 Tabs and Drop-Down Menus

You should note that all the instructions in this chapter are designed for Word 2007. Some folks may still be using Word 2003, which is fine; Word 2003 can do all the APA formatting functions that Word 2007 can do. However, the menus and the screen shots look different; in other words, the organization and appearance of the features changed from 2003 to 2007, but all the functionality remains if you are still using Word 2003. For Mac users, some of the Office for Mac functions are a little different.

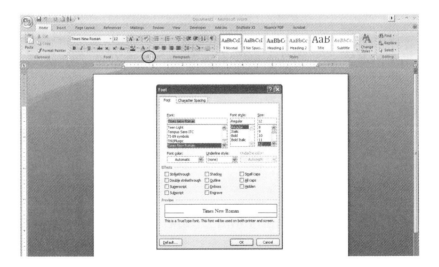

This is the header bar at the top of Word 2007 screens. In this screen shot, you may see choices that are not on the version you are using; don't worry about that. We've installed some "add-ins" for our versions of Word that you won't need for preparing APA-formatted papers. (For example, *Nuance PDF* is a cool program that converts a PDF made by someone else into a Word file that you can edit—very handy at times.) See what is circled in the preceding graphic. Word is organized on the basis of tabs listed across the top of the screen. Your tabs probably look like this: *Home—Insert—Page Layout—References—Mailings—Review—View*—and perhaps other add-ins if you have them. Clicking on a tab presents many other options and choices, which will appear just below the lineup of tabs.

There are certainly other methods of accessing particular functions in Word, including shortcut keys and drop-down menus. You can access some of the menus that look like Word 2003 menus in the Word 2007 program. For example, if you were to click on the item circled in the graphic that follows, you would get the *Font* drop-down menu much like you see in Word 2003. Sometimes these complete menus can be handy if you have to make a set of complicated changes, such as changing the font size, font, and other details for more control. If you just need to change one feature quickly (e.g., just the font alone), the tabs across the top of the page work very well.

Setting the Margins

APA format is very consistent about margins: 1-inch margins on all four sides of the paper (top, bottom, right, left). If you set your default document properly, you will never have to change the margins. But you should know how to anyway, because you might be swapping documents with classmates or merging two files into one. To set the margins, start by clicking on the *Page Layout* tab indicated in the next graphic.

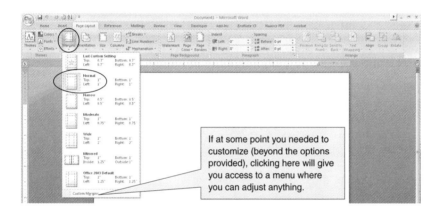

When the page layout options appear, click on *Margins*, and then click on *Normal*; the drop-down box also indicates that *Normal* is 1-inch margins on all four sides of the paper, which is exactly what you want for APA format.

If at some point you needed to customize (beyond the options provided), clicking here will give you access to a menu where you can adjust anything.

Line Spacing and Spacing Between Paragraphs

Throughout the text of your APA-formatted paper, you'll need to use double-spacing. If this is not how your default document opens in Word you'll have to change it for the document you are working on. Click on the *Home* tab and then on the icon circled in the next screen shot; when you hover over it (i.e., leave your cursor over it for a second), a box will show that it is called *Line spacing*.

Clicking on the *Line spacing* icon will give you access to the drop-down box presented next. For double-spacing, select 2.0—which stands for double-spacing.

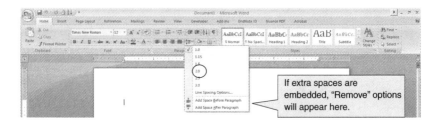

If extra spaces are embedded, "Remove" options will appear here.

Sometimes in Word 2007, you will see extra spaces between paragraphs; in APA format, you do *not* want this. You want regular double-spacing throughout the entire document, with no extra spacing added, for example, between paragraphs. There are at least two ways to fix the extra spacing. If there is extra spacing between paragraphs, the drop-down box presented in the previous screen shot will have the option *Remove Space Before Paragraph* or *Remove Space After Paragraph*. Clicking on the relevant choice is one way to remove the extra space. Another way to remove the extra space is to use the more complete (Word 2003) drop-down menu shown in the next screen shot. There shouldn't be any need to use the *Add Space* option if the rest of the formatting is correct.

You can get quick access to the drop-down box by clicking on the icon in the circle in the next screen shot. Make sure that under the heading *Spacing*, both *Before* and *After* are set at 0 pt.

Then, in the *Line spacing* section, change the current selection (in blue) from *Single* to *Double*, which will give you double-spacing. If you want that to apply to the entire document, press Ctrl+A before choosing *Double* on the *Line spacing* menu, and the entire document will be double-spaced. As you can see, typically, you can achieve formatting changes in Word 2007 in one of several ways. You don't necessarily have to do it the way we are showing you here, but we want you to know of at least one method that you know (and we know) that works! Also in this box, you can remove the extra spaces between paragraphs by making sure it says 0 pt in the boxes labeled *Before* and *After*.

Page Headers (First Page and Subsequent Pages) and Page Numbering

To be honest, the page header system is a bit confusing and difficult to master at first. The page header (the information inside the top 1-inch margin of your APA-formatted paper) is different on page 1 than it is on the remaining pages of your paper. So here, through a series of screen shots, we'll show you how to make the page 1 header different from the headers in the rest of in your document. This is one of the most common questions we have from our students; by getting this down, you'll be way ahead of the game.

The easier part is to insert the page number, which will appear in the same place on every page of your paper; you also want to make sure that the inserted page number matches the font you are using—usually Times New Roman 12-point font. To insert the page number in the header, start with the *Insert* tab and then click on the *Header* selection (highlighted by the circle in the next screen shot).

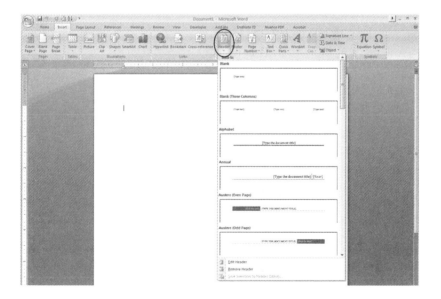

Because you have multiple tasks to achieve in the page header, rather than do these one step at a time, you can access menus that allow you access to greater control where you can achieve many steps at one time. Under the *Insert* tab and keeping with the *Header* selection, choose *Edit Header* instead; see the circle in the next screen shot.

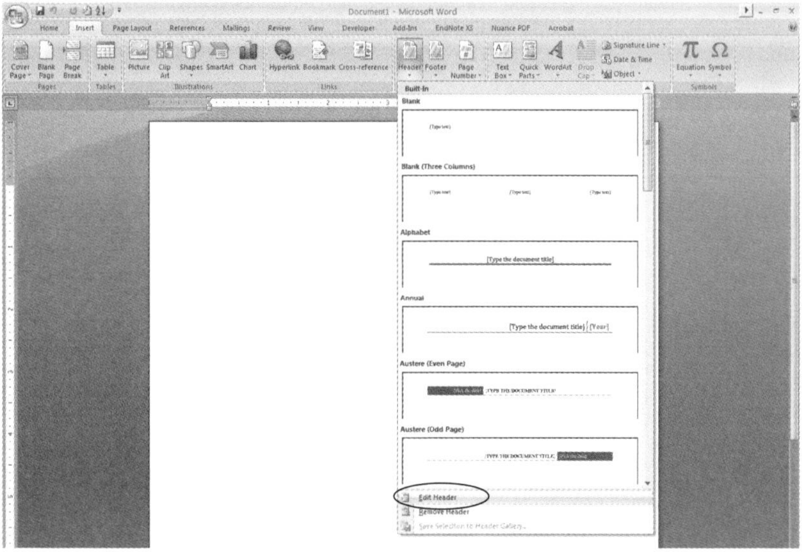

When you click on this option, a whole new set of advanced controls is now available to you, called *Header & Footer Tools* (see the very top line of the screen shot, shaded).

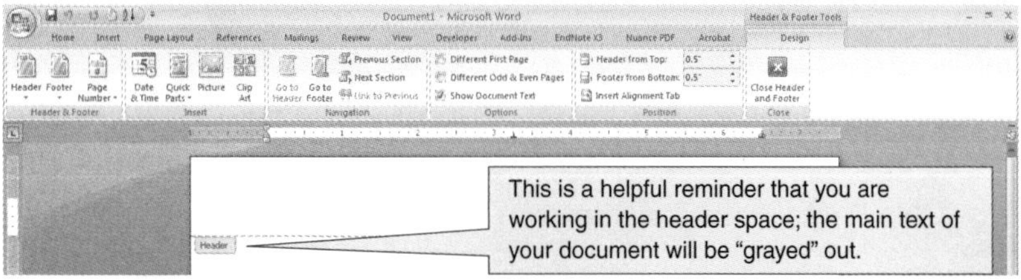

This is a helpful reminder that you are working in the header space; the main text of your document will be "grayed" out.

First, insert your page number, which must appear in exactly the same place on every page. As you can see in the next screen shot, first place your cursor exactly where you want the page number to appear (rightmost margin inside page header, using tabs or the keyboard shortcut Ctrl+R), click on *Page Number* as seen in the graphic, then on *Current Position* (circled), and finally, click in the first box, labeled *Simple* followed by *Plain Number*. That will insert the page number, and you won't be inserting any more page numbers. This feature will automatically number every page in the file, and the number will automatically change for you when you add or subtract pages.

On the first page of an APA paper, inside the top 1-inch margin, the words "Running head," followed by a colon, should appear followed by a short title in all capital letters (50 characters or less, including spaces). On every subsequent page of the manuscript, only the short title (i.e., without the Running head label) in capital letters appears at the top of the page inside the header region. To differentiate the first-page header from all the other page headers, click on the option labeled *Different First Page*, circled in the next screen shot.

On page 1, you'll include the Running head indicator, followed by a colon, followed by the short title (in CAPS), with the page number at the end of the line, but on page 2 (and all other pages) you'll have just the short title (in CAPS) with the page number at the end of the line. The sample paper in Chapter 19 provides a nice illustration of this feature in actual use.

Tabs, Centering, and the Ruler

Typically, the default tabs in Word 2007 will work just fine—one-half inch (0.5″) with each time you press the tab key. You can gain greater control over tabs, and centering as well, but first you'll need to make sure you are viewing the ruler, because the ruler is essential for setting tabs. In the next screen shot, there is no ruler, so we'll show you how to activate it.

You'll want to press the small icon on the rightmost side of your screen a little below the large options that appear above your document (when you hover over it, you'll see that the icon is labeled *View Ruler*). Click on that (circled).

You will see that two rulers appear—the horizontal ruler at the top of the page (you'll use this one the most) and the vertical ruler down the left side of the page.

One method of inserting tabs is to use the tab icon circled in the previous screen shot; you can rotate through different types of tabs (by clicking repeatedly on this icon), and then place (and move) them on the ruler. To be honest, this isn't the easiest to do; the more complete menus from Word 2003 are also available for this function.

To access the more complete drop-down menus, click on the icon circled in the *Paragraph* section of the *Home* tab as shown next, and then select the *Tabs* . . . button at the bottom of the menu.

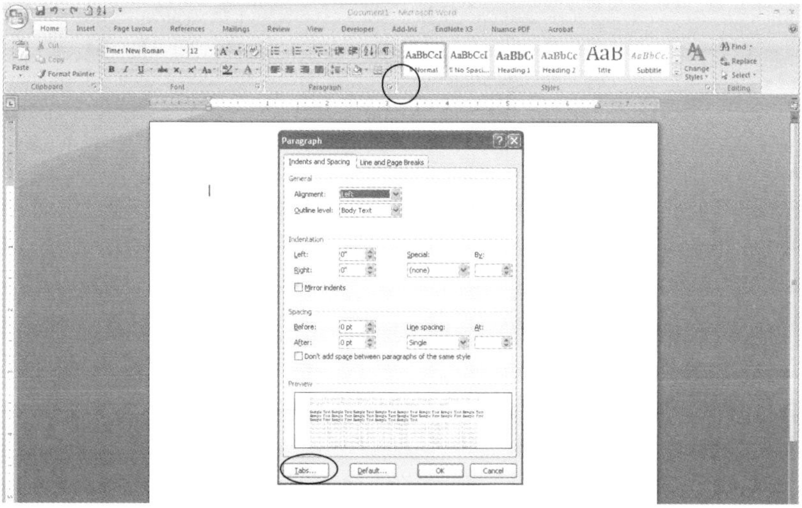

Now you can set your tabs with precision, using exact locations rather than the drag-and-drop feature with the ruler bar. The alignment feature can be handy when you are trying to line up decimal places for a table. Although you probably will not use this in an APA-formatted paper, say an instructor asked you for a table of contents, with a dotted line leading to the right where the page number is listed. To accomplish that function, you would use the drop-down menu on the next graphic. Under *Leader*, you could select the type of line you want to use to "lead" the reader across the page to the page number (in a table of contents).

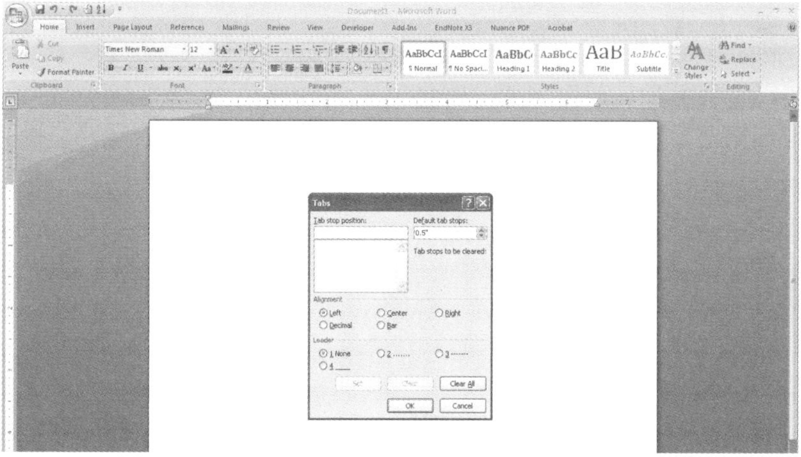

Centering using Word is very straightforward. Typically, you highlight with your cursor what you want to be centered (or even place your cursor within the word you want centered), and then you click on the button in the *Home* tab circled in the next screen shot. Sometimes this is trickier than you might think. If you have a tab (indent) on the line and you type in your heading (Method, for example), this centering feature will center **Method** with the 0.5-inch tab included—meaning that the Method section heading really isn't centered at all. Make sure there are no other tabs or spaces on the line that you wish to center. One easy way to watch for this is to click on the paragraph symbol in the *Home* menu, shown in the next graphic. This now reveals within the text of your paper where there are spaces and all other pagination symbols so you can easily spot spaces.

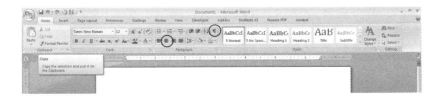

One more problem that occasionally occurs with student papers (which is easily fixable) is when you accidentally hit the wrong formatting button. In the next screen shot, you can see that the button circled looks like it might be used to center, but it is really for justification (right-justification, specifically). Right-justification means that Word will insert spaces along the line in between words so that the right margin will be exactly even; this is the way most newspaper columns look. You do *not* want this in APA format; instead, you want your paragraphs to be left justified, with a jagged right margin. If you hit the *Align Text Right* justification button by mistake, you can (a) click on the *Undo Typing* icon (the backward-facing arrow on the far left end of the tool bar); (b) highlight what is justified and hit the *Align Left Text* button (to the left of the *Centering* button); or (c) press Ctrl+Z, which works the same as clicking on the *Undo Typing* icon.

References and the Hanging Indent

Your References section will appear toward the end of your APA-formatted paper; it starts at the top of its own page (you can easily achieve this by inserting a page break; see this tip a little later in this chapter). References are double-spaced just like the remainder of the paper, but they have a special format, called a "hanging indent." The first line of the reference is flush left, but all the subsequent lines of the reference are indented. You do *not* want to insert a bunch of spaces or tabs to achieve this, because if you do, and then you have to reformat your paper, you'll have to redo the formatting for every individual reference. Believe us, we've learned this the hard way. There is an efficient shortcut trick to doing this.

First, type all your references in APA format, including double-spacing, proper italicization and capitalization for titles, and correct punctuation—all this without the hanging indents (see Chapter 10 for reference styles). The next screen shot shows an example of a book reference before formatting. Hit *Enter* at the end of each reference, as if to start a new paragraph. In fact, you can type in all your references this way and then use the hanging-indent trick once (after you "select all" by pressing Ctrl+A), or you could use it on individual references. (Don't worry about the squiggly lines underneath the author names. Word doesn't recognize those as properly spelled words, but that's OK; the squiggly lines will not print.)

Then, change the references format into the hanging indent appearance; just highlight all the references with your mouse as indicated in the next example.

With all the references highlighted, let go of the mouse and press Ctrl+T on your keyboard; you will see the hanging indent as you do on the next screen. Click anywhere in the document, and the blue highlighting will go away. You are now ready to resume your other writing tasks, with the hanging indents of your references easily achieved. If you have to copy and paste or change reference styles later, the hanging indent will remain; you don't have to add or subtract spaces or tabs to achieve the hanging-indent effect.

Preparing a Table (Rows, Columns, Lines, Centering)

Depending on the type of writing you are doing for an instructor, you might need to prepare a table. Tables are very precise in APA format, and there is a section of your *PM* dedicated to preparing tables. You can also find additional books (e.g., Nicol & Pexman, 2010) that will give you tips on how to prepare a basic table. Here, we'll just get you started with the basic Word commands to start a table; you can see an example of an APA-formatted table at the end of the sample paper in Chapter 19 and more instructions on how to create tables for data in Chapter 13.

If you know the size of the table you want to insert (i.e., the number of rows and columns needed), you can start on the *Insert* tab, click on *Table*, and then *Insert Table*, circled in the next screen.

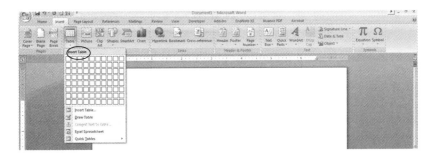

Drag your cursor across the matrix of rows and columns presented, and when you let go of the mouse button, it will insert a table of those dimensions into your Word document. For example, in the next screen, the cursor has been dragged to make a 3 × 5 shape, and you can see the three columns and five rows that were inserted into Word.

From this table, you still have much formatting to do. Space here does not permit step-by-step instructions, because the rules are very precise (but you can see an example table at the end of the sample paper in Chapter 19). To format your table, click anywhere inside it, and an entire new set of tools will emerge— *Table Tools.*

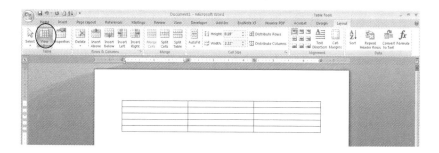

From this menu you will be able to erase the lines you do not want and draw the lines you do want in a table. For example, in a properly APA-formatted table, there are no vertical lines. In the previous screen shot, four vertical lines need to be removed. As you remove the drawn lines, you will still see the outline of the table displayed as gridlines; dotted blue lines show the shape of the table, but the lines will not print. To properly format your table, make sure you are using gridlines; to do this, select the option labeled *View Gridlines,* circled in the next screen shot.

As you change the characteristics of different rows and columns, you can right-click on a cell or row or column, and a context-specific drop-down box will appear, as in the next screen shot. A number of handy table-editing features are available to you in the drop-down box, such as inserting a row or column, deleting a row or column, merging cells, aligning text within cells, changing the measurements (dimensions) of rows and columns, or seeing how tables break across pages. As we mentioned previously, these details only scratch the surface of what you can do with the tables feature in Word. Even though this may be a bit daunting, learn how to use it. Do *not* prepare tables by drawing in lines by hand or by using tabs. Show your instructors that you are learning to master the tools of your trade.

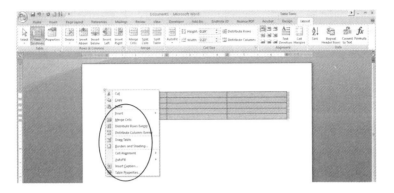

Fonts and Font Variations (Italics, Bold, Superscript)

Technically, there are three levels of Word formatting—the font level, the paragraph level, and the section level (Krieger, 2005). Section-level formatting can be very useful in Word, but it is probably not necessary for the APA papers you will be preparing. Given that you'll be using the same font throughout your paper, font-level formatting will be perfectly appropriate for you. Most of the time, just accessing the Font section (circled in the next graphic) from the *Home* tab will achieve most of the functions you need.

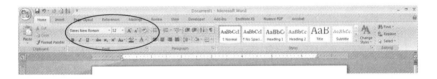

In those cases where you may need a bit more control or options for special features of font sets, you can access the more complete Word 2003 menu by clicking on the icon circled in the next screen shot.

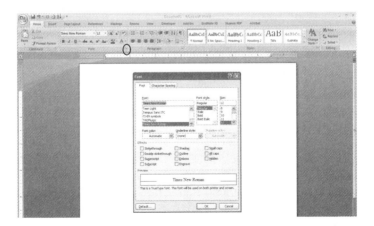

Page Breaks, Orphans, and Widows

Certain parts of an APA-formatted paper start at the top of the page, such as the Abstract, Introduction, References section, and each table. On the other hand the end of the Method section just flows with regular double-spacing into the Results section. At the end of the Discussion section, the References section (which follows Discussion) starts at the top of the next page. To start a new page, you could just hit *Enter* a bunch of times on your keyboard, or you could insert a page break, which will move the cursor immediately to the top of the next page. Just as you can insert page breaks, you can remove page breaks as well. To insert a page break, all you need to do is access the *Insert* tab and then select *Page Break* (circled in the next graphic), or you can use the keyboard shortcut Ctrl+Enter. An easy way to remove a page break is to backspace from the line following the break.

Widow and orphan control is another feature you should be sure to use. The setting described here and mentioned in Chapter 19 will help keep text together in a document. For example, if the Results section heading in a research paper is "alone" at the bottom on the page (no other text underneath the heading on that page), you should insert a page break to push the heading to the top of the next page. That type of separation is called a "widow"—that is, when a heading for a new section or the first line of a paragraph is separated from the text that follows the heading or from the rest of the paragraph. Even though adding a page break to move the "widowed" Results section heading to the top of the next page may leave a large margin at the bottom of the previous page, this is preferable to separating the Results heading from the rest of the Results section. Another type of formatting to keep in mind concerns the very last line of a paragraph that appears at the top of the next page of your document. This type of separation is called an "orphan." In this context, avoid orphans and widows. Most of the time, the *Widow/Orphan* control box, when checked, does a good job of keeping first and last lines of paragraphs on the same page, but occasionally you may have to insert a page break to avoid widows. The next screen shot shows you where to find the *Widow/Orphan* control box.

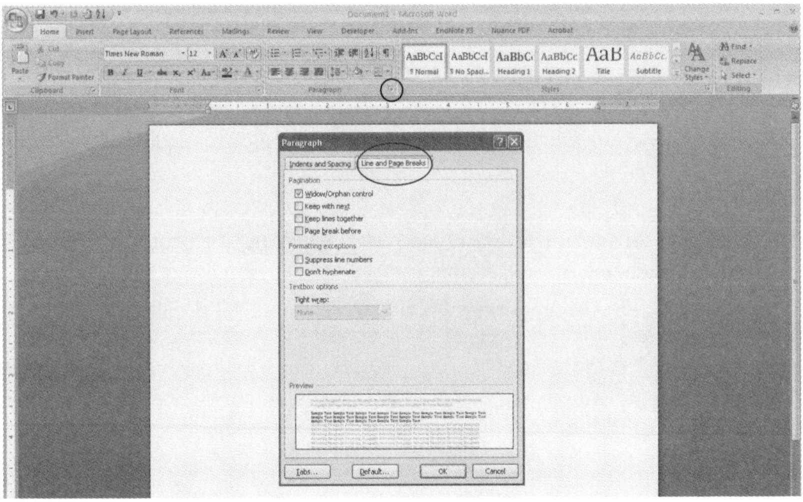

Spell-Checker and Grammar Checker

Although they're not perfect, we recommend that you use the spell-checker and the grammar checker that accompany Word. Suspected spelling errors will be identified by a squiggly red underline, and suspected grammar errors will be identified by a squiggly green underline. Hovering the cursor over the identified item and right-clicking should bring up a context-specific box where suggested replacements are offered. On those occasions when you know you've spelled a word correctly, you simply click on *Ignore* and the squiggly line will go away.

To make sure these features are activated, click on the *Office* button as indicated in the next screen shot; then click on the *Word Options* button at the bottom of the menu, which will bring up the display you see next.

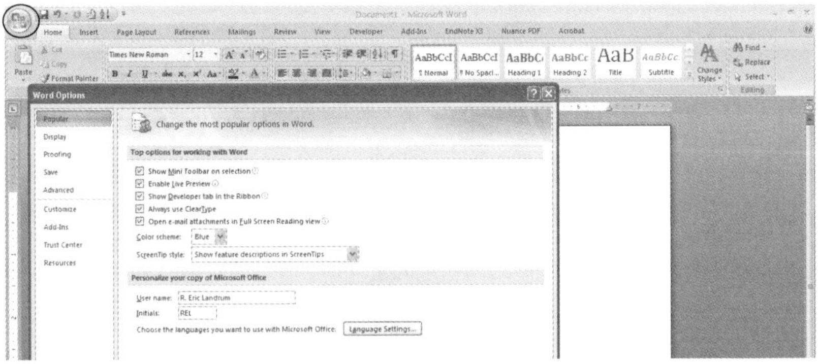

To make sure your spell-checker and grammar checker are activated, click on the *Proofing* option (circled in the next graphic), and select the spelling and grammar options you want.

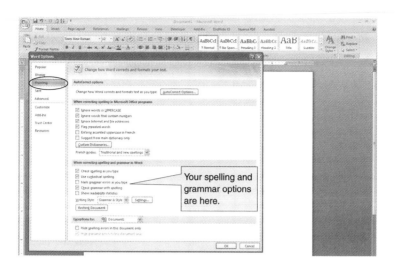

Note that this feature will not catch all spelling and grammar errors; you are responsible for your own work, especially proofreading it. Many other parts of this book (including Chapter 18 on proofreading) can help you avoid those obvious mistakes that can be irritating to your instructor when grading, and you want to avoid that. After you've worked on a paper for a while, it might be hard to find your own mistakes, so swap with a classmate; offer to proofread his or her paper while your classmate proofreads your paper. A new set of eyes can do wonders for finding errors that you've looked at over and over again.

Developing Good Habits: Autosave, File Naming, File Storage, Frequent Backups

One of the important details of using powerful tools such as Word 2007 is letting the tools help you do your job better. Part of that process is the ability to save and retrieve your work. That might sound like a simple task, but have you ever lost a file? Has the power ever gone off while working on a computer, or has your laptop battery died unexpectedly? Word provides an autosave feature that can minimize work losses; you may have seen these auto-recovery screens before when you rebooted your computer after a power loss. Starting from the *Office* button (circled in the next graphic), select the *Save* option and review what you have checked there. You can see that the default is 5 minutes for autosave; that is, if the computer crashed, the most that would be lost is 5 minutes worth of work. But if you are a speed typist and can crank out 500 words in that time, that might be too much work to risk. You have the option of making the minutes value smaller—say, saving every 3 minutes. You can also have the backup files saved to a web location if you don't want to save backups to the hard drive you're working on.

By paying attention to a few more details, you can make your interactions with this powerful Word tool go more smoothly. First, use descriptive file names; you will be able to figure out what's in the file faster, and any search engines you use to find files will have to search only the file names and not internally in each file (which could be a slow process). Be systematic about your file names. When working on a paper with multiple drafts, save each draft with a different file name; it could be "Developmental psychology paper Version 1.1," "Developmental psychology paper Version 2.0," and so on. Or embed today's date into the file name, and that way you'll have an additional guide to knowing what day you worked on what draft of the paper. It is also a good idea to include your last name as part of the file name. This becomes helpful if you need to submit your paper electronically. Your instructor would probably prefer not to have a classful of papers titled "Developmental Psychology Paper."

Be consistent where you store your important files; perhaps they are always on your laptop or copied to a trusted USB memory stick/flash drive. If you establish some consistent file storage routines, you will spend less time looking for where your work *is* and more time actually working on your paper. If you work on many different computers throughout the week, you might want to think about using a large USB drive or perhaps an external hard drive designed for travel. Finally, you have to back up your files on a consistent basis; we recommend at least once a week. Pick a convenient time; maybe every Thursday morning you will back up your hard drives while you are getting ready to go to class. Once a month, back up your backups. These are all mechanical devices, and they will eventually fail. You do not want to experience that sinking feeling of putting hours and hours into a paper or project only to find out all that work is lost and now you'll have to re-create it; that's not an efficient use of anyone's time. Develop a consistent backup procedure now and invest in some backup hardware; you'll be happy you did later. If you can learn and master these tools of the trade, writing in APA style (knowing the rules and proper formatting) will allow you to concentrate on the psychological story you wish to tell.

SECTION V

Some Nitty-Gritty Details

Making a List, Checking It Twice 15

Enumeration and Seriation

E ver had that argument when you were so ticked off you spouted off at the mouth and could not wait to get all those reasons you were mad off your chest? Perhaps you wanted to tell someone who wronged you all the reasons you were right and he or she was wrong. Well, in scientific writing, there are also times you have much to say. You have hypotheses to support, findings to list, possible explanations to line up. For each of these reasons, regardless of which section of your paper you are writing, you need to know the APA rules on the different ways to order, list, and present your ideas. Knowing how to list in APA style is a useful skill to have. Knowing how to properly list items using APA format might even encourage you to use lists more often (if appropriate).

Why Bother?

Knowing how to order your points in a series, hence the word *seriation*, is a key writing skill that enables your reader to better understand your main ideas. Many individuals may not have heard the actual term before but still have presented ordered lists of information. Seriation is designed to make your key points clear. The problem is, and the three of us have seen many examples of this, many writers use a variety of erroneous techniques to present lists. We have seen students use different fonts, different font colors, and even different font sizes to order points (remember, your entire paper should be the same Times New Roman 12-point font). We have also seen students use a variety of symbols and bullets. Word may have some funky symbols for use, but they do not belong in an

APA-style paper. Another consideration: Be careful with lists and seriation. Too many lists in a student paper can make it look like the student did not really write the paper but instead cobbled together a bunch of lists. Our advice is to use lists sparingly, and when you do use a list, follow the seriation rules precisely so that you can show your professors your attention to detail.

Keeping Order at the Section Level

An empirical paper is organized into major sections such as Introduction, Method, Results, and Discussion. The Method and Results sections have their own natural order of presenting information and normally do not require seriation. For example, the Method section has the Participants, Apparatus or Materials, and Procedure sections. However, you may want to order steps when describing your procedure, or you may want to have a list of conclusions in your Discussion section. A variety of options are available for including lists in your APA paper. You just need to be sure you use the appropriate labels for the list that you chose to include.

When your lists are separate sentences or separate paragraphs, you use numbers (not Roman numerals) followed by a period and with each sentence in the series ending with a period, not a semicolon (;) or comma (,). You do not need to use parentheses "(1)" or even "1)" either. Several seriated paragraphs would look like this, as seen below.

A variety of first-year seminars exist on a wide range of college campuses. Barefoot (2005) classified freshman seminars into five major types:

1. Extended orientation seminar. Sometimes called a freshman orientation or student success course. It often covers issues of campus resources, time management, academic and career planning, and other topics.

2. Academic seminar with generally uniform academic content across sections. An interdisciplinary or theme-oriented course, which may be part of a general education requirement. Focus of the course is on the academic theme but will often include academic skill components such as critical thinking and writing.

3. Academic seminars on various topics. Similar to number two above, except the academic content varies from section to section.

4. Pre-professional or discipline-linked seminar. Designed specifically for students within a specific major or discipline.

5. Basic study skills seminar. Offered typically to academically underprepared students. Focus is on basic skills such as grammar, note taking, and test taking. (Gurung & Wilson-Doenges, 2010, pp. 97–98)

Now sometimes you may look at a list like the preceding one and assume, because of the numbers, that the first item is better than the second one and much better than the last one. To avoid this tendency, you can use a bulleted list instead of a numbered list. If you are submitting your paper to a journal for publication, the "look" of the bullet will depend on the style used by the journal. For a class paper assignment, it is best to use either small squares or circles. We know this seems designed to squash your individuality, but keep in mind that the creative ideas emerge in the content of your paper and in the way you combine ideas rather than in your font choice or the size of your margins. There are better battles to fight. Go ahead, be square. Or don't (use the circles). We do not see too many student papers that require a bulleted list or that even use one, but it is nice to know what you can do if you so choose.

Order Within Paragraphs or Sentences

If you do not use seriated paragraphs too often (or have never even thought about doing it), you will probably have more use or more occasion to seriate within a sentence. In this case, you need to use lowercase letters enclosed in parentheses (APA, 2010a). The simple version looks like this:

> In a comprehensive, nationwide study, Landrum, Gurung, and Spann (2010) assessed how student attitudes toward (a) learning, (b) their textbooks, and (c) their instructors influence their own learning as measured by exam scores.

In the example above, none of the segments following the letter in parentheses (e.g., learning, their textbooks) have commas themselves, so the three parts are separated by commas. If segments of a sentence do have commas, then you need to separate them by semicolons. Let's tweak the sentence to illustrate what this would look like.

> In a comprehensive, nationwide study, Landrum, Gurung, and Spann (2010) assessed how student attitudes toward (a) learning, school, and success; (b) their textbooks, computers, and notebooks; and (c) their instructors influence their own learning as measured by exam scores.

Although most instructors likely prefer the seriated examples just presented, you could also use bullets to separate out the elements of a sentence. In this case, because all the bulleted items are still one sentence, you treat it for exactly what it is—a sentence. Hence, there is only one period at the end. Again:

> In a comprehensive, nationwide study, Landrum, Gurung, and Spann (2010) assessed how student attitudes toward

- learning, school, and success;
- their textbooks, computers, and notebooks; and
- their instructors

influence their own learning as measured by exam scores.

On a Related Note

There are a few other circumstances when you have to order items. If you have to order a set of tables or figures, the enumeration of these items is discussed in Chapter 13. You may decide to use footnotes, information that expands on information in the main text of your paper (but that you think would be of interest to only some readers). As a matter of fact, few undergraduate student APA-style papers need to use footnotes (and not just because many students want to use all the text they can to get to their assigned paper length). If you do use footnotes, number them in the order you use them, identify them with a superscripted number, and then either include the corresponding numbered footnote text at the bottom of the page where you need it or order all your footnotes on a separate page at the end of your paper. Unless your assignment requires footnotes, here is our advice: Avoid footnotes at all costs!

It may appear that much of this chapter is a cosmetic flourish. In some ways it is, but good seriation and accurate enumeration can make a long list of information much easier to comprehend.

The Devil Is in the Details 16

Abbreviations, Signs, Symbols, and Punctuation

When most people think about APA style, they may imagine it has to do with the technical aspects of psychology and science. The fact that APA style has ways to cite sources, write a reference section, and describe data is understandable. Not as many people recognize that APA style also relates to the somewhat smaller things in life: abbreviations, signs and symbols, and punctuation. Once you have graduated from elementary school, you may think that you have punctuation down. From the way we have seen simple punctuation misused, especially commas and exclamation points, we recognize that some guidance cannot hurt and can make papers stronger. In this chapter, we address some of those underappreciated paper components; remember, for some instructors, it's all about these details. Given that many of these rules will be common knowledge for most of you, we use more of a checklist-like format in this chapter (also see Chapter 4 for more on punctuation).

OMG: To Abbreviate or Not?

We've all used abbreviations in everyday life, whether in e-mails or text messaging. We have BFFs and often LOL (best friends forever, laugh out loud), and sometimes we may even exclaim in abbreviated form (*#@!*; you fill in the blanks). Clearly, *these* abbreviations do not belong in an APA-style paper. Many others do. There are a number of types of abbreviations, such as Latin and scientific abbreviations, and there is a simple tip to a clear paper: Limit the use of abbreviations. If your paper is packed with abbreviations, your reader may stumble. Ask yourself if you really need them. A good rule of thumb is that if you will not use the word too often, not more than three times, do not abbreviate unless the abbreviation is for a very long term (APA, 2010a). If, for example, you are using a questionnaire with a really long name (e.g., Multidimensional Body Self-Relations Questionnaire), you may want to use the abbreviation after the first use of the questionnaire name. Specifically, you *must* spell out the full name the first time you use it, followed by the abbreviation in parentheses; after that, you can use MBSRQ in the rest of the paper. Sure, one may think that abbreviations make your paper look technical and impressive, but abbreviations are more likely to confuse than impress.

Now here is something you may not have known. There are abbreviations listed in the dictionary that look like regular word entries (e.g., REM, AIDS, HIV). You do not need to explain these or spell them out, and the *PM* does deem it acceptable for you to use any such abbreviations in your papers. OK, so it will probably be faster for you to type out the abbreviation than to check a dictionary to see if it would be OK not to spell it out, but we thought this was an interesting quirk to share anyway.

Blinding You With Science and Latin

We talked about statistical abbreviations in our chapter on reporting data analyses in your Results section (Chapter 9). The rules for the use of scientific and Latin abbreviations are similar. Most Latin abbreviations (for example, "e.g."), which we use in abbreviated form naturally, are used only within parentheses. If you want to use the same phrase outside parentheses, you should use the English translation, which of course means you should know what the translation is. A major exception is the Latin for "and others," et al., which is always written in the Latin whether within parentheses or not (APA, 2010a). Don't forget the period after the "al."; et al. is actually an abbreviation for the Latin phrase "et alia."

When using scientific abbreviations such as those for time and units of measurement, some basic rules apply. Abbreviate all units that follow or are used with a number, and if using a series of numbers, you need to use the abbreviation only after the last number in the series.

> **Incorrect:** Students in the three conditions drank 5 ml, 10 ml, and 25 ml of high-caffeine soda, respectively.

> **Correct:** Students in the three conditions drank 5, 10, and 25 ml of high-caffeine soda, respectively.

The exception is certain units of time (day, week, month, and year), even if they are accompanying numbers. Those terms are never abbreviated. All other units of time are abbreviated. Table 16.1 presents the most typical abbreviations you are likely to use.

Table 16.1 Some Common Abbreviations and Their Meanings

Abbreviation	Meaning
etc.	and so forth
e.g.	for example
i.e.	that is
cf.	compare with
vs.	versus
hr	hour
min	minute
s	second
°C	degrees Celsius
°F	degrees Fahrenheit
g	gram
IQ	intelligence quotient
L	liter
m	meter
a.m.	ante meridiem
p.m.	post meridiem

Some other dos and don'ts:

- Don't start a sentence with an abbreviation in lowercase—or with any abbreviation if you can help it.
- Add an *s* to make an abbreviation plural (no apostrophe needed).
- Do not make an abbreviation of a unit of measurement plural (e.g., 5 min, 100 mg).

Punctuation

By the time you reach college, most of you have written a fair number of papers. In college, you often have to take composition or expository writing classes. In most of these classes, you learned how to use punctuation well. This next section presents the major punctuation rules to keep in mind for APA style:

- **Use** one space after all punctuation, including periods—except when periods are used in abbreviations (e.g., a.m., p.m.) or to end sentences in a draft paper; APA now suggests two spaces after a period at the end of a sentence in a draft paper.
- **Do not use** periods for abbreviations of state names (e.g., WI, VA, ID) or capital letter abbreviations (e.g., APA, APS, IQ).
- **Use** a comma before the *and* or the *or* in a series of three or more items (e.g., Tom, Dick, and Harry).
- **Use** a comma to set off a descriptive part of your sentence. **A tip:** If you took the descriptive part out, the sentence should still make sense. Try this tip with the following sentence, and also look at your sentences that have more than one comma in them:

  Correct: I always take my good luck shirt, a colorful bowling shirt in black and blue, with me on holiday.

- **Limit** your use of exclamation points (!); in fact, in formal writing (such as an experimental paper), you shouldn't use an exclamation point at all.
- **Limit** your use of dashes (—). More often than not, a comma or semi-colon will work.
- **Use** double quotation marks to set off buzz words or coined expressions, titles of articles mentioned in text, and examples from a questionnaire:

  Correct: Eric really "raised the roof" with tales of his high jinks.

- **Do not use** double quotation marks for key terms; use italics instead.

There is more to know about punctuation of course, some of which we discuss in Chapter 15 on seriation and enumeration.

SECTION VI

In Closing

Important Considerations

Using Rubrics 17

Knowing What It Means to
Write a Good Paper

In this chapter, we hope to present two strong points: To improve your work, (a) follow rubrics when provided, and (b) avoid common errors in APA style and format. Writing improvement comes with practice (and more practice and still more practice), and you will have evidence of your enhanced writing skills as you learn to make fewer errors and tell a clearer story when writing in APA style.

Follow Rubrics When Provided

As a student writing a paper in APA style, you might be feeling that it is a logistical nightmare to make sure you've followed all APA rules. After all, who would have thought you would need to know whether to use spaces between numbers when including an equation in your paper? If possible, imagine having to grade these papers! We know what you're thinking: "I would rather grade them than have to write them!" When we describe how these papers are graded, you might just change your mind. This chapter will help you better understand the way many professors grade APA-style papers and how this approach can help you avoid common errors and receive a higher grade on your assignments.

To help provide clear expectations and grading criteria for an assignment, to create a fair and unbiased grading system, and to provide detailed feedback to students, many instructors use grading rubrics. What is a rubric? A grading rubric provides students with detailed information on what the instructor is looking for when grading assignments and how grades will be determined. Typically, rubrics include qualities and descriptors for each performance standard and a point system that indicates how well a part of your paper fits the predetermined rubric guidelines; essentially, it is the scoring system that the instructor will use to grade your work. Implicitly, this scoring system communicates what is important in an assignment and the most difficult parts of the assignment. For instance, if you were writing a research paper including actual data, the instructor might decide that the Introduction section is worth 100 points, but the Method section might be worth 25 points. The higher point value might indicate that the Introduction is more important, more complicated to write, or both. Whenever possible, ask instructors if they would be willing to share any grading rubrics they may be using. Rubrics come in all shapes and sizes. Your best bet is to read over the criteria very carefully to make sure you understand what is expected. Read carefully the description of what is included in the rubric and understand the guidelines before you start to write your paper. After you read over the rubric, ask questions you have about any part of the rubric (i.e., ask your instructor for clarification). Then, after you've written a first draft, go over the different parts of the rubric, and as honestly as possible, compare your paper to the grading criteria. Pair up with a classmate and compare each other's paper against the rubric. The following is an example of a rubric you might see when writing different parts of an APA-style paper.

Example Rubric

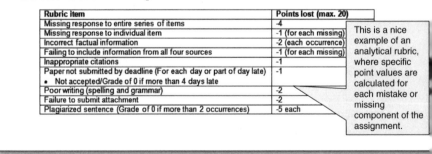

Grading Criteria: You will earn the full 20 points for each paper if you meaningfully address all required items, include appropriate citations for factual information, write using grammatically correct sentences and proper spelling, write using your own words (avoiding plagiarism), complete and submit any related questionnaires (e.g., a Body Shape Questionnaire for the Hunger assignment) with your paper, and submit your paper by the deadline. Points will be deducted for the following:

Rubric item	Points lost (max. 20)
Missing response to entire series of items	-4
Missing response to individual item	-1 (for each missing)
Incorrect factual information	-2 (each occurrence)
Failing to include information from all four sources	-1 (for each missing)
Inappropriate citations	-1
Paper not submitted by deadline (For each day or part of day late) • Not accepted/Grade of 0 if more than 4 days late	-1
Poor writing (spelling and grammar)	-2
Failure to submit attachment	-2
Plagiarized sentence (Grade of 0 if more than 2 occurrences)	-5 each

This is a nice example of an analytical rubric, where specific point values are calculated for each mistake or missing component of the assignment.

The preceding analytical rubric is from Dr. Pam Marek's (Kennesaw State University) General Psychology syllabus. You can find more rubric examples at Project Syllabus, which is part of the Society for the Teaching of Psychology website: www.teachpsych.org/otrp/syllabi/syllabi.php). Better still, if you're curious about rubrics and want to make your own, check out Rubistar (http://rubistar.4teachers.org/). What is useful about Dr. Marek's rubric is that you have specific explanations beforehand about what the instructor will be "looking for" when grading, and the point values do imply which mistakes are more heavily weighted. Thus, if you received 12 of 20 points, by reviewing your work you should have a clear indication of why you lost points in particular parts of the writing assignment. Importantly, this review of the rubric and the points you received will also tell you what part of the paper you need to focus on even more for future assignments. Again, this type of rubric is called an analytic rubric because it provides specific criteria for different parts of a paper. In contrast, you might be given a holistic rubric, which does not separate grading criteria for the different parts of a paper and therefore may be less definitive in spelling out how many points a mistake is worth. An instructor using a holistic rubric relies on a global perception of quality rather than an accounting of mistakes. With either system, it is always important to pay attention to the rubric *before* turning in your assignment; ask questions if you are unclear about what a plagiarized sentence is or if you need an example of being too colloquial. And be sure to value and follow the feedback that instructors provide to you. We suggest you go through each comment made on your paper; if you are unclear about any suggestion provided to improve your writing, set up an appointment with your instructor for clarification.

Get It Right!

Proofreading the Entire Paper

18

We know how exciting it is to finally finish writing a paper. You just want to step away from the computer and perhaps never see it for a while (or ever again if it was a tough one). Although we encourage you to take a break, we also urge you to leave time for proofreading your paper at least once before handing it in. The difference between a proofread paper and one that isn't may be the difference between receiving the grade you worked hard for and the grade you hoped to avoid. If you are tired of proofreading your own paper, then swap with a classmate; trade proofreading for proofreading. A fresh set of eyes looking at your work is a good idea in any case. Ask any professor who grades papers, and he or she will tell you how frustrating it can be to see minor errors in a paper, especially repetitive errors. These minor errors can be so much of a nuisance that they are often included as part of the grading rubric or they simply may be one component of the paper considered when grading without a rubric. At the end of this chapter, we include some sample pages where we have purposely embedded many APA errors. How many can you find? We encourage you to test your APA knowledge and find the errors. To check how many you were able to find, compare what you found to the list of errors in Appendix A.

Why is proofreading necessary? We've all been there. When writing a paper, we usually focus on the content to create logical arguments and paragraphs that include thoughts that flow smoothly from one sentence to the next. The components of the assignment run through our head. Thoughts such as, "Don't forget you need to include at least five references" or "How can I be sure this will be between eight and ten pages in length" are distracting. With all that going on, you are left with little mental energy and attention to focus on the details, which is particularly true if you have limited time to complete your assignment (do not procrastinate; start early!). But even when time is available, it is easy to overlook misspellings, punctuation mistakes, and grammatical errors, not to mention all the APA format and style rules. Perhaps we have convinced you at this point that proofreading is a good idea.

Convinced or not, we offer some foolproof steps to take when proofreading your paper. A key factor in proofreading that needs to be stated up front is the time needed to make this process work. You need to build in the time to write multiple drafts of your paper; in other words, writing assignments completed at the last minute leave no time for proofreading and review. You are wasting your time when someone reviews your paper and you don't give yourself the time to incorporate the feedback and comments into an improved draft. Some students make the cardinal error of asking an instructor to please comment on a draft, and then they don't make any of the changes that the instructor spent time and energy to provide. Not making changes based on feedback can be very frustrating indeed for the instructor. We can all tell you that few people write an error-free paper on a first draft. Even your professors continue to write multiple drafts of the papers they are writing when submitting their work for journal reviews or submitting paper submissions for a conference. First, leave time between your writing and your proofreading. You might have had the experience of writing a paper and just feeling wiped out. Rather than proofing in that state, you are better off taking a look at your paper when you can reread it with "fresh eyes." Sometimes it is hard to make changes to a paper that you've just worked many hours to write and in turn feel that there is no need for changes. Time between writing and proofing can make all the difference.

Next—and this may seem obvious to many of you—we strongly recommend that you use the spell-checker tool and the grammar check tools. Don't rely on those squiggly red, green, and blue lines to find errors. It is very common to mentally fill in the missing letters or change words to fit the sentence (i.e., perceive things that are not really there) when reviewing a paper simply because of our experience with the English language. This leads us to overlook errors. One easy way to find some mistakes is to read your paper slowly out loud. The words that are not misspelled but do not fit the sentence will pop out when you actually hear the sentence spoken rather than reading it to yourself (e.g., "Writing in APA style is always fan"). This way, you are more likely to identify awkward phrases, extra words, or misused words. In fact, you might consider reading out loud to a friend who can help you find awkward-sounding sentences. Better yet, you could have the friend read your paper out loud to you, in which case you might hear something different from what you thought you had written. When it comes to grammar, one surefire way of finding grammatical errors is to read your paper for each type of common error. These errors include sentence fragments, subject-verb agreement errors, unclear pronoun references, run-on sentences, words you've typed twice, words you've completely left out, and your use of apostrophes.

Here are a few suggestions for searching your reference list for three common errors:

- The period after an author's initial before the ampersand should be followed by a comma (e.g., Landrum, R. E., & Gurung, R. A. R.). Search for a period followed by a space followed by an ampersand (. &), and add the missing comma after the period before the ampersand.
- Search for a closing parenthesis followed by a space; unless the parenthesis is part of a title, it should be followed by a period or a comma, depending on where it is in the reference (that is, the ending parenthesis after the publication date is followed by a period; the ending parenthesis after "Ed." or "Eds." in a reference for a chapter in a book is followed by a comma).
- Search for a comma before an opening parenthesis and delete it; a comma should not appear before an opening parenthesis in a reference.

Keep in mind that although proofreading can mean reading your own paper to remove errors, it can also mean having someone else proofread to find the errors that you as the writer might overlook. After you've spent all that time and energy working on a paper, it is difficult to imagine that you've made mistakes. That is exactly why it is in your best interest to have someone else take a look at your paper before handing it in to your professor. Of course, because we're not talking just about proofing for grammar and logic but also for APA style and format, it would be best to have someone with knowledge of APA guidelines and requirements do the proofing. But who? Sometimes this is determined for you, with peer review included as an assignment in your class; that makes it easy to find someone to read your paper and also provides an incentive for additional proofreading. However, even when it is not included as an assignment you might consider making a deal with someone else in your class—the old "I'll scratch your back if you scratch mine," though you'll be reading papers instead of scratching backs. Well, we suppose some back-scratching could be involved too. To increase the chances that the proofer is reading with specifics in mind, you might consider giving your proofreader a copy of a rubric from the class or even the list generated from Chapter 20 that covers the most common APA errors.

Whether it is you or someone else proofing, you want to make sure that the paper is read with the audience in mind. Proofreading your paper will be most effective when you switch from reviewing your paper as the writer to reviewing your paper as a reader. Of course for most of you, the audience will be the person who assigned the paper. Using the rubric, as mentioned in Chapter 17, can definitely help with keeping the audience in mind, the expectations provided by your instructor, and what differentiates a strong paper from a weak paper. Just so you know, each of the three authors of this book read each draft of these chapters a number of times before we let anyone else even see them. Over and over. Again and again . . .

Although some like to review papers using a printed copy, the easiest way to obtain feedback for your paper is by using the Track Changes tool in Word. See the next graphic.

Simply click on the *Review* tab and then on the *Track Changes* option, and you can provide feedback within the paper, letting the author know when any changes have been made.

Another helpful tool when proofreading is the *Comment* option, also available under the *Review* tab. Using this tool, you can write comments in the margins of the paper to let the author know something about the paper without making a mark within the paragraph itself. Be sure to save the document with your comments and changes, using a new file name to differentiate it from the original draft. We find that adding the date and your initials is an easy way to keep track of multiple drafts of any paper under revision.

When you are unable to find someone to review your paper, you should also consider using a resource available on many campuses—the writing center or writing lab. These centers include professional staff members and/or peer tutors who have been trained to assist students with writing. Some centers even train their tutors in APA style and format. One of the best uses of this center would be to bring along the grading rubric you received to make the reviewer aware of the expectations for this assignment. That will allow the reviewer to really focus on the details and what differentiates a strong paper from a weak one.

Then there is the paid source of feedback always available through the Internet. We have never tried this ourselves, but we've seen the offers out there. Remember, if you are going this route, you need to make sure that the reviewer knows you are writing an APA-style paper. You know for yourself how an APA paper differs from other papers. You certainly don't want to pay someone to suggest changes to your paper that are not in accordance with APA style. There are sites that are specific to writing in APA style, and plenty of YouTube videos to show you how to format papers for APA style. So if you learn APA style and format well enough, you have just opened up a career option you never dreamed about—editing APA-style papers. We also suggest that you check with your instructor regarding the use of this type of resource. At some schools with honor codes, it is not acceptable to use this type of help on any work. In particular, note that we are *not* suggesting you pay someone to write your paper. You obviously need to do your own work.

So when do you know you have proofed your paper enough? If you've reread your paper and/or had someone else read your paper over at least one time, you've checked your paper against the rubric for the assignment, you've gone through the checklist provided at the end of this book that gives you a list of the most common APA style and format errors, and the deadline is here . . . it's time to stop proofreading and hand in your paper! Or e-mail it as an attachment. Or deliver it to your instructor following the preferred method.

As we mentioned earlier, the next section of this chapter includes sample pages from a paper with *many* APA errors. You'll be surprised how easy these errors are to miss the first time you review these pages. We encourage you to try this exercise and note the errors that are easy to find when proofreading a paper and the ones that are easy to overlook (see the answer key in Appendix A). Determining the ones that are easy to miss when using this sample paper can help remind you what style and format rules to not overlook when reading your own paper.

Sample Student Paper for Practicing Proofreading

The Pharmacological Effects   1

The Pharmacological Effects of Caffeine

Cire Murdnal

PSYC 101 Section 001

April 21, 2011

The Pharmacological Effects of Caffeine

Caffeine is probably the most consumed psychoactive substance in the world (Graham, 1978). Interestingly, its origins derive from all parts of the world as well. Caffeine exists naturally in a number of forms, including the coffee bean, kola nut, cocoa bean, ilex (holly) plant, and from the cassina or Christmas berry tree in North America (Stephenson, 1977). The coffee bean was first found in Arabia, the tea leaf in China, the kola nut in West Africa, the cocoa bean in Mexico, the ilex plant in Brazil, and the cassina in North America.

Caffeine is currently consumed in a number of forms, including coffee, tea, cocoa, cola beverages (pop), chocolate, and it ts often used in a number of over-the-counter preparations, such as Dexatrim, Anacin and Vivarin. Unless consciously monitoring caffeine consumption, most Americans consume from 200-250 m.g. caffeine daily, and many may not even know it. (Stephenson, 1977; Graham, 1978)

Caffeine is an alkaloid compound which belongs to a class of drugs called methyl xanthines. The technical (chemical) structural name for caffeine is 1,3,7-trimethylxanthine. Two other closely related compounds also exist in the methylxanthine group, theophylline (1,3-dimethylxanthine) and theobromine (3,7-dimethylxanthine). Both are naturally occurring substances, theophylline commonly found in tea, and theobromine found in tea and cocoa (Graham, 1978).

The Pharmacological Effects   3

In terms of sources of caffeine for use in naturally
consumed foods and caffeine-enhanced preparations (cola
and over-the-counter medications), caffeine most commonly
originates from coffee (Coffee arabica), tea (Thea sinensis),
chocolate (Theobroma cocoa), and kola (as in the kola nut) (Cola
nitida). When crystallized and removed from the natural source,
caffeine is water soluble, odorless, and definitely bitter (Graham,
1978).

According to Curatolo and Robertson (1983), caffeine
is essentially completed absorbed (more than 99%) from the
gastrointestinal tract after oral administration. While some reports
vary peak plasma levels occur about 30 minutes to 1 hour after
ingestion (Curatolo & Robertson, 1983; Stephenson, 1977). The half
life of caffeine in the system does vary due to individual differences,
but the average half life is about 3 hours (Stephenson, 1977),
although in some individuals the half life of caffeine has been
reported as high as 7.5 hours (Curatolo & Robertson, 1983). Clearly,
some individuals are more caffeine-sensitive than Others. The
distribution of caffeine throughout the human system occurs rapidly
and thoroughly; within minutes, caffeine enters all organs and tissues
and has its effects in proportion to the amount of caffeine present
(the more present, the greater the stimulatory effect) (Graham, 1978;
Stephenson, 1978).

The pharmacological actions of caffeine occur on the cellular level.
Caffeine's primary site of action is probably through the antagonism of
adenosine receptors. A secondary site of action is the caffeine also works

as a phosphodiesterase inhibitor. Phosphodiesterase is an enzyme necessary to convert cyclic AMP (cAMP) to AMP. Methylxanthines in general, and caffeine in particular, inhibit the process of enzymatic degradation allowing for the continued stimulation of cAMP at the cellular level (Robertson, Curatolo, & Robertson, 1983; Stephenson, 1977).

The rate of metabolism of caffeine has been found to be about 15% per hour. Even in high doses (e.g., 500 mg/day), there has been no demonstration of day-to-day accumulation of the drug (Stephenson, 1977). Although multiple metabolites the primary metabolite of caffeine is 1,7-dimethylxanthine. The metabolites chiefly follow a renal route for excretion (Curatolo & Richardson, 1983).

On the cellular level, caffeine metabolism leads to increases in muscle lactic acid, increased oxygen consumption, and muscle twitches (Stephenson, 1977). Other larger, behavioral effects are briefly discussed elsewhere in this paper. The primary route of excretion is through the kidneys. Most of the renal metabolites are passed in the urine, but small amounts have been reported to have been excreted from saliva, semen, breast milk, and caffeine has heen found in blood from an infant's umbilical cord (Graham, 1978; Curatolo & Richardson, 1983). From 0.5% to 3.5% of caffeine will exist unchanged, mostly in the urine but small amounts will exit via the feces (Curatolo & Robertson, 1983).

The clearance of caffeine from the system can be altered by other circumstances, however. For example, caffeine clearance (elimination) slowed by alcoholic liver disease (alcoholism) and

The Pharmacological Effects   5

clearance is also slowed in the newborn. Caffeine clearance is accelerated with concurrent smoking (Curatolo & Robertson, 1983).

The cardiovascular effects of caffeine are mixed. While caffeine stimulates cardiac muscle which in turn leads to increased force of contraction, increased heart rate, and increased cardiac output, caffeine also stimulates are portion of the brain called the medullary vagal nuclei which in turn decrease heart rate. These opposing actions may result in bradycardia, tachycardia, or no change in the consumer (Stephenson, 1977). In addition, brain blood vessels are constricted and brain blood flow is reduced. These actions may help to explain why caffeine can be effective in headache relief, and why "caffeine headaches" often appear as withdrawal symptoms in those curtailing their consumption of caffeine.

Caffeine has found to be a general stimulant in terms of metabolic effects. In other words, caffeine itself acts as a trigger for starting or accelerating the rate of general metabolism. Many weight-loss regimens have taken advantage of this phenomenon and included caffeine for its stimulation of metabolism and diuretic effects (Curatolo, Robertson, 1983).

Another major metabolic effect of caffeine is the increased release of glucose after caffeine consumption. It has been well documented that caffeine has a hyperglycemic action (Stephenson, 1977), and this helps to explain why the occasional candy bar or can of Coke acts

as a pick-me-up: a quick boost of glucose available for the
brain.

Caffeine also effects the CNS by influencing the
processes of psychomotor coordination, EEG patterns,
sleep, mood, behavior and thought processes. For
instance, caffeine has been found to decrease reaction
time and increase vigilane in relatively straightforward
laboratory tasks. Use of caffeine before going to bed
can increase sleep latency (the amount of time needed
to fall asleep), decrease total time asleep, and decreases
subjective estimates of sleep quality (Curatolo &
Robertson, 1983).

Caffeine has also been found to effect mood, behavior, and
cognitive processes (hence its justification as a psychoactive drug).
Caffeine users have reported increased perceptions of alertness, increased
ability for short-termed behavioral activity, and relatively minor changes
in cognitive processing (Curatolo and Robertson, 1983). Although
effects on cognition appear to exist (hence the worldwide popularity and
desire to use the drug), surprisingly little empirical evidence is available
demonstrating its influence. Other than effects on vigilance, reaction time,
alertness and sleep patterns, caffeine's effects on behavior have been
elusive in the laboratory.

References

The Pharmacological Effects   7

Curatolo, P. W. & Robertson, D. (1983). The Health Consequences of Caffeine. *Annals of Internal Medicine, 98,* 641-653.

Graham, D. M. (1978). Caffeine—Its identity, dietary sources, intake and biological effects. *Nutrition Reviews, 36* (8), 97-102.

Stephenson, Phillip. E. (1977). Physiologic and psychotropic effects of caffeine on man. *Journal of the American Dietetic Association, 71,* 240-247

Complete Sample of an Experimental (Research) Paper

19

Samples, Anyone?

This chapter is all about samples. It is one thing to go over the rules of APA style and format with you and translate what the *PM* means to what you need to know for your scientific writing. But you also need to see the APA rules in practice. In this chapter, we present the research paper you might have already seen in Chapter 2. Jessica Kesler (2010) of Boise State University graciously gave us permission to reprint her paper here again to point out features of APA style and format. In Chapter 2, you saw a visual table-of-contents using this same sample paper. In that chapter, we pointed out the details about APA style and format and where to find a discussion of those details in subsequent chapters. In this chapter, we include the same sample paper, but this time we spell out the rule.

We have kept each page proportional to how it would look after you printed it out; in other words, we know you are not reading this on a piece of 8½ × 11-inch paper, but that is the size paper *you* will print on. So the graphics in the paper included in this chapter are to scale. We purposely chose this approach so that you get a close approximation of what your final APA papers will look like, proportionally speaking.

To be honest, sometimes instructors add to the confusion of writing in APA style (for more on this, see Chapter 17). In the instructions in your syllabus, it might say "prepare a 5–7 page paper in APA format." Unfortunately, that assignment is vague. Is that five to seven pages of text? Does the page count include the title page? The references? If it is not an experimental/research paper, does the instructor want an abstract? (Typically not.) So after you receive the instructions for any writing assignment, you have to translate, decipher, and interpret what the instructor really wants. What exceptions to APA style does he or she prefer? It may seem like you are being picky with your questions, but you'd rather be picky on the front end and know exactly what is expected of you than be surprised at the back end with an unusually low grade because you didn't understand the instructor's preferences. We get it that sometimes this arrangement isn't fair, but if you will be proactive and follow our advice, you can minimize those surprises, which are disappointing.

So as you look at the formatting and read Jessica's paper on the pages that follow, you'll see that she had to make certain adjustments to conform to the assignment in her Research Methods class. For example, she reported nonsignificant results in her Results section; in published papers, that doesn't happen too often, but practicing data analysis and reporting techniques were part of the course goals. This assignment also required a minimum of six references and had to include a table. So aspects of the sample paper you see in this chapter may not be part of a writing assignment you must complete. The number one rule to remember is to write for your audience; in many cases, the audience for your writing is also the person with grading responsibilities.

One last thought before digging into the paper: This is a real student paper. Parts of it have been modified from the original, but this is meant to be a realistic example of student work. Is it a perfect paper? No (and Jessica is OK with that). Will you find errors or mistakes in the paper? Probably. We selected this paper as an example or template, but not as an exemplar of perfection. Moreover, the point is not to look for errors, but to see if the author is telling a coherent and meaningful story. The goal is not to look for mistakes as if you are on a treasure hunt, but to read for the scientific story. Does the story make sense, and is it compelling? Along the way of reading the scientific story, you'll also see a brief description of an APA style or format rule that you need to keep in mind when writing your own paper. Telling a coherent scientific story that communicates a meaningful message is a difficult enough task; adding the many APA writing details is a whole different task in itself. If you'll follow the advice provided throughout this book, you'll be well on your way to knowing those many details and in turn you will be able to focus your attention on honing your scientific storytelling abilities.

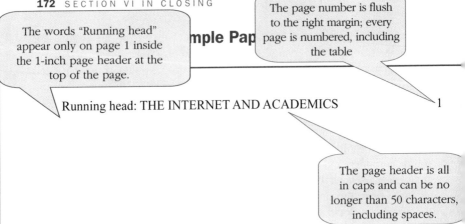

mple Pap

The words "Running head" appear only on page 1 inside the 1-inch page header at the top of the page.

The page number is flush to the right margin; every page is numbered, including the table

Running head: THE INTERNET AND ACADEMICS   1

The page header is all in caps and can be no longer than 50 characters, including spaces.

Problematic Internet Use and the Effect on Academic Performance

Jessica T. Kesler

Boise State University

Title should be no longer than 12 words. Double-space everything. No course number on title page unless specifically instructed to do

THE INTERNET AND ACADEMICS   2

The Abstract heading is centered and not boldfaced. Make sure you don't center this line with a tab embedded; otherwise, the label will not be truly centered.

This is the page header on all remaining pages (no "Running head" as on page 1).

Abstract

I examined the relationship between Internet usage (specifically, social networking sites) and student grade point average (GPA). Using 8[...] 8 college students participated in the study. There [...]t difference between a participant's year in school and [...] social networking sites belonged to. There was also a significant relationship between the amount of time the participant spent on the Internet on how frequently they found themselves browsing the Internet for enjoyment when they should be using the Internet for school-related subjects. Continued monitoring of student trends in Internet use is warranted to better understand how students can maximize efficient usage of time resources as well as meet the goals of staying socially connected.

Keywords: social networking sites, Internet, college students

The Abstract is not indented and should [...] no longer than 120 words.

Keywords aid in the identification of articles when searched for in a database. These are the types of terms that you insert in your PsycINFO search.

THE INTERNET AND ACADEMICS 3

Problematic Internet Use and the Effect on Academic Perfo[...]

College in[...]utions worldwide have come into the

twenty-first [...]ury by making the *Internet ava*ilable in many [...]

their c[...]es. In fact, the Internet is so accessible that studen[...]

[...]t over studying, potentially sacrificing their grad[...]r a few

entertainment. Altho ugh the Internet makes [...]lable a

[...]dge that students can use, Internet use prese[...]s opportunities

to distract users from being productive (Kraut, Patterson, & Lundmark, 1998).

Although the Internet is considered a good resource by many, too much of

anything may be harmful. According to Ozcan and Buzlu (2007), healthy

Internet use is "use of the Internet for an expressed purpose in a reasonable

amount of time without cognitive or behavior discomfort" (p. 768). By letting

one's Internet use effect academic success, you may no longer hav[...] grasp

healthy Internet use (Ozcan & Buzlu, 2007).

Researchers at Ohio State University completed a pilot stu[...]

on the effects of social networking sites (specifically Facebook) a[...]

academic performance, and concluded that college students who [...]

popular social networking site Faccbook spend less time studying [...]

have lower grade point averages (GPA) than their peers who have [...]

joined Facebook. Furthermore, the typical Facebook user has a G[...]

about 3.0 to 3.5, whereas non-Facebook users had GPAs between 3.5 and

4.0 (Karpinski & Duberstein, 2009). The differences in GPA could be

linked to the number of hours a week spent studying—5 hours for users,

compared to 11 to 15 hours per week for nonusers. But the authors of this

study did not draw the conclusion that using social networking sites leads

to lower grades, and that possibly other factors like personality, could

link Facebook usage and lower GPA. Pempek, Yermolayeva, and

Annotations:

Inside parentheses an ampersand (&) separates the last author from the second-to-last author.

The title from page 1 reappears at the top of page 3. The word Introduction is not used as a heading. Do not boldface the title.

A direct quo[te] requires cita[tion with] the page num[ber or] paragraph n[umber] from the sour[ce] which the ma[terial is] quoted[.]

THE INTERNET AND ACADEMICS   4

...e that if it wasn't for Facebook, some ...ays to avoid studying, and would still ...e lower GPAs could actually be because ...time socializing online" (p. 236).

...ternet too much ca... ...ge from mild ...t issues and social iso... ...o more ...eep disturbance, dep... ...al symptoms in association with excessive ti... et al., 1998), Although some of these symptoms ap... a drug or alcohol addiction, according to Scherer (1997), one cannot be physiologically addicted to the Internet the way one might be to drugs and alcohol, but using the Internet excessively can lead to similar dependent behavior and cravings. Kubey, Lavin, and Barrows (200... 13% of college students have Internet dependency probl... also a relationship between online procrastination and ... Internet use. Studying these two concepts addresses the po... ...lack of self-control over the time spent on the Internet and t... ...ck of ability to acknowledge the distraction and entertainment th... Internet can provide. In a study by Thatcher, Wretschko, and Fridjhon (2008), these researchers found a strong correlation bet... use and procrastination because the Internet p... ns of stress relief and entertainment, making p... arly since individuals possess the ability to look ... d, although potentially not academically engaged at all.

The goal of my study is to partia... y replicate the previous pilot from Ohio State University (Karpinski & Duberstein, 2009), and expand

> With three to five authors, the second time (and all other times) you cite the work, use the first author's last name, followed by et al., which is the Latin abbreviation for et alia, meaning and others." If the reference has six or more authors, use et al. the very first time citation appears in the paper as well as on each subsequent appearance.

> Minimal use of abbreviations is recommended; always be sure to define the concept completely before using the abbreviation.

> With multiple authors mentioned outside parentheses, use the word *and* between the second-to-last and last author.

> With only two authors, list both authors completely each time cited.

THE I

> This is a great use of the first-person pronoun here. Framing the sentence this avoids passive voice. The passive voice sentence would be "It was hypothesi that . . ." The action is with the researcher, and she did the hypothesizing, so not say so?

upon the knowledge about the impact of internet us on academic

> In an experimental paper, the introduction section ends with specific, testable hypotheses. This is followed by the Method section, with the heading centered and boldface

cause of use of the Interne r procrastination.
from a pool of Boise State University general
were then asked to complete a survey regarding
their Internet habits and academic progress. I hypothesize that the
more time a student ds using the Internet, the lower the student's
GPA. I also hypothesize th the more social networking sites belonged to,
the lower that person's GPA hypothesis of this study is that the more time
a person spends on the Internet, the more often they would be browsing
the Internet for fun when they should be using the Internet for academic

Method

> For each of the subheadi in the Method section (Participants, Materials Procedure), the subheadi boldface and flush left, a appears on its own line

Participants

There were 118 participants in this study; 60 women, 47 men,
and 11 participants not reporting sex. Participants were general
psychology students who enrolled for participation using the web-
based program Experimetrix. The average age was 20.84 $(SD = 6.04)$.
The sample consisted of 75 freshmen, 26 sophomores, 5 juniors,
2 seniors, and 10 participants who did not report year in schoo
Participants in general psychology were rewarded with course c it
for their participation.

Materials

> Statistical sy are italicized example SD for star deviatio

Participants responded to eight questions relating to their In
use and their academic success. I created these questions, and the
were pilot tested prior to being administered to the participants. Pleas

THE INTERNET AND ACADEMICS   6

see Table 1 for a list of questions presented to participants by this study,

including overall means and standard deviations.

Procedure

> Some abbreviations are predefined by APA format, such as min for minutes; note that a period does not follow the abbreviation, unless at the end of a sentence.

The eight questions used in th. (omnibus) survey that consisted of 23. ...questions. Participants were

tested in groups and given 50 min to complete the survey. On average,

> If this Results heading (boldface, centered) had originally appeared at the bottom of the
> evious page, you would "push" it to the top of the next page. Even though that may leave
> arge margin at the bottom of the previous page, the large margin is preferable to separating
> the Results heading from the rest of the Results section. That type of separation is called a
> *idow*—when the first line of a section is separated from the rest of the section on the next
> ge. An *orphan* is when the last line of a paragraph appears at the top of the next page, all
> alone. In this context, avoid orphans and widows.

Results

In reference to the first hypothesis predicting that the more time

> viding the scales
> a item correlated,
> lp the reader to
> better sense of
> the correlation
> ually means.

ends on the Internet, the lower the grade point average

nducted a correlation between answers to the item "how

do you use the Internet during an average week (for both

...entertainment purposes)" (answered on an interval/ratio

scale) and answers to the item "what is your current GPA" (answered

on a scale from 0.00-4.00). There was a statistically significant negative

correlation between answers to the survey items, $r(59) = -.28, p = .028$.

The second hypothesis is that the more social networking sites

one belongs to, the lower the GPA., regardless of gender and year in

school. Answers to the item "how many social network   ites do

you belong to, i.e., MySpace, Facebook, Twitter" were co   d with

answers to the GPA question. There is not a significant c

between number of subscribed social networking sites and

$r(71) = -.01, p = .936$.

> This is APA format for a correlation. The *r* is italicized, followed by degrees of freedom in parentheses, then the actual *r* value to two decimal places, followed by the exact *p* value.

This phrase "the third hypothesis" is a nice signpost for the reader to help keep track of the story's progression.

The third hypothesis is that the more time a person uses the Internet, that time is spent more for fun that for academic purposes. I explored Internet usage using answers to two survey questions: "how many social networking sites do you belong to (i.e., e, Facebook, Twitter, etc." (answered on an interval/ratio) w many hours do you use the Internet during an average

The verbal descriptors for survey scale scores are always italicized.

Using a (1) and a (2) like this is called seriation. To be APA compliant you would use letters—(a) and (b)—instead of numbers in parentheses.

r both acade   answered on val/ratio scale
two   ne/frequency m   the answers o these two Likert   agreement (1 = *strongly disagree* to 5 = *strongly agree*) items: (1) I find that my use of the Internet interferes with my ability to get good grades, and (2) I believe that my Internet use causes me to procrastinate on my studies. Number of social networking sites was not significantly correlated with answers to the item "I find that my use of the Internet interferes with my ability to get good grades $r(100) = .13, p = .196$. Numher of social networking sites was significantly posifives correlated with answers to the item "I believe that the Internet causes me to procrastinate on my studies," $r(99) = .22, p   .028$. Time on the Internet was significantly positively co lated with answers to the item "I find that my use of the Interr interferes with my ability to get good grades," $r(83) = .2   p = .031$. Time on the Internet was not significantly correlate   ith answers to the item "I believe that my Internet use cau   me to procrastinate on my studies, $r(79) = .15$,

The correlation is reported to two decimal places, with rounding. The exact probability level is reported to three decimal places. When $p < .05$, we would reject the null hypothesis. The exact p level indicates the probability of that r value with that many degrees of freedom by chance alone. Thus, with 102 participants ($df = N - 2$), you would expect to get $r = .13$ by random chance alone 19.6% of the time.

THE INTERNET AND ACADEMICS 8

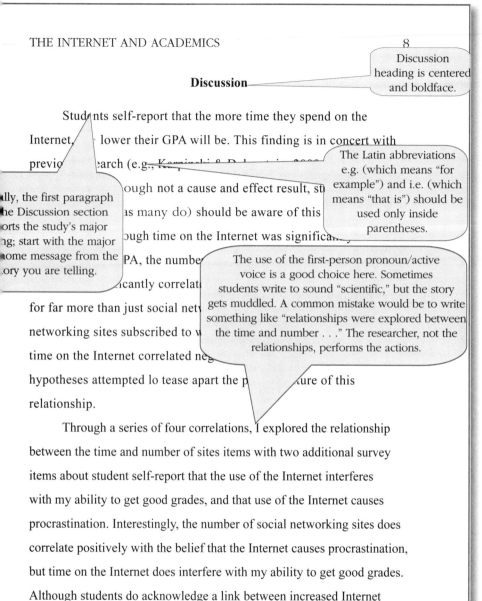

Discussion

> Discussion heading is centered and boldface.

Students self-report that the more time they spend on the Internet, the lower their GPA will be. This finding is in concert with previous research (e.g., Kaminski & ...

> The Latin abbreviations e.g. (which means "for example") and i.e. (which means "that is") should be used only inside parentheses.

... though not a cause and effect result, st... as many do) should be aware of this ... ough time on the Internet was significa... PA, the numbe... ...icantly correlat... for far more than just social net... networking sites subscribed to w... time on the Internet correlated ne... hypotheses attempted lo tease apart the p... ...ure of this relationship.

> ...lly, the first paragraph ...he Discussion section ...orts the study's major ...ng; start with the major ...ome message from the ...ory you are telling.

> The use of the first-person pronoun/active voice is a good choice here. Sometimes students write to sound "scientific," but the story gets muddled. A common mistake would be to write something like "relationships were explored between the time and number . . ." The researcher, not the relationships, performs the actions.

Through a series of four correlations, I explored the relationship between the time and number of sites items with two additional survey items about student self-report that the use of the Internet interferes with my ability to get good grades, and that use of the Internet causes procrastination. Interestingly, the number of social networking sites does correlate positively with the belief that the Internet causes procrastination, but time on the Internet does interfere with my ability to get good grades. Although students do acknowledge a link between increased Internet time and lower GPA/poorer grades, they do not limit this perception to the use of social networking sites. Rather, students report their increased use of social networking sites as a mechanism for procrastination, but not relating to grades.

THE INTERNET AND ACADEMICS   9

'These findings coincide with the Ohio State University pilot study

hypothesis that the average student who did not ~~

11 to 15 hours studying, whereas a student with

5 hours studying (Karpinski & Duberstein, 2009)

> Normally, the number 5 would be spelled *five*, but because a number precedes a measure of it is written as a numeral and a word.

that those who spend less than 5 hours online may spend more time

studying, and those who spent between 21-25 hours on the Internet

were studying very little. The goal of this study was not to a complete

replication of Karpinski and Duberstein (2009), but to expand upon the

idea that involvement in any social networking site (not just Facebook)

has an effect on participant GPA. I was unable to replicate the findings

demonstrating social networking's effect on GPA, but I did find a

significant correlation between the number of social networking sites a

participant belonged to and their level of procrastination. One possible

danger here for students is that they may not realize that too much

procrastination (that is, too much social networking) may ultimately

impact grades and GPA, even if students self-report that they believe no

relationship exists.

    Results reported by Thatcher et al. (2008) coincide with the

significant differences found in this study between the number of hours

a participant spent on the Internet and how often the participant found

themselves browsing the Internet for enjoyment instead of academics.

The study conducted by Thatcher, et al. (2008) echoed the idea that the

Internet provides people with a means of procrastinating. The relationship

between online procrastination and problematic Internet with the

issue of lack of self control over time spent on the I

acknowledgment of the distraction the Internet can

2008).

> Even though the Thatcher reference has not been cite a while, et al. is still appropriate because all the authors were the first time cited.

THE INTERNET AND ACADEMICS   10

The results of this study confirm in a speculative manner that Internet

usage does vary between ~~stud~~ that more social networking and

In the Discussion section, if you are going to speculate about the possible
meaning of your results, it is best to be fair and label your ideas as
speculation. In fact, when reading any paragraph in a research paper
like this one, if no citation is listed somewhere in the paragraph,
it will be assumed that all the ideas in that paragraph belong to the
paper's author. If you do not give credit where it is due, that's
plagiarism, and you must avoid that.

Every research study
has limitations,
which usually appear
toward the end of the
Discussion section.

of the Internet, should be a continuing focus of study. For example

procrastination early in an assignment timeline has little to no effec

assignment performance, but procrastination prior to the assignment d

date has more substantial effects. Understanding when Internet use fo

pleasure and social networking is a key determination that students   st

make in order to also achieve academic goals.

The limitations of this study were the limited number of questions,

as well as some of the written questions. It would be advantageous to

continue studies over time to see if changes in GPA A are sensitive to the

time constraints (or lack thereof) regarding Internet usage. The Internet is

a very present technology in society. With over half of the United States

population with home Internet access (U.S. Census Bureau, 2   ), the

Internet makes available a wealth of knowledge that p   can use, but

it also poses a threat to a person's productivity (al., 1998). It is

clear from experience and from data gath   he course of this

stud   f time spent

may   at benefit

to th   f social

netw   uals may

The closing paragraph to a research study has
three goals: (a) to remind the reader of the take-home
message, (b) to remind the reader of the importance of
this study in filling a void in the literature, and (c) to
remind the reader of the importance or magnitude of the
overall topic.

prosper from appropriate usage.

THE IN

> The Reference section should start at the top of its own page, with the References heading centered (but not italicized).

> Typically, there is somet italicized in every AP reference: a book title, name of a journal, the v number for a journal, the name of the webpa

References

Karpinski, A., & Duberstein, A. (2009, April). A *description of Facebook use and academic performance among undergraduate and graduate students.* Presented at the annual meeting

> The doi stands for "digital object identifier"; not every journal article will have one. This is a feature that helps to provide a permanent link to journals available online, even though websites can change.

> This is a conference presentation which differs from the typical jour book, or Internet reference. Note inclusion of the month of presentat as well as the name of the confere and the city and state where the conference was held.

psychological well-b .. *American Psyc.*

doi:10.1037/0003-066X.53.9.1017

> Notice the capitalization rules for journal article titles. The only words that are capitalized are the first word, the first wor after a colon, and proper nouns. The sam capitalization rules are used for book title

> Use an ampersand (&) between the last author and second-to-last author for all reference citations.

Barr
ance d
2. doi:10.11 466.2001.tb02885.x

Ozean, N. K., & Buzlu, S. (2007) net use and its relation with the psychosocial situation a sample of university students. *CyberPsychology and Behavior, 10,* 767-772. doi:10.1089/pb.2007.9953

Pempek, T.,
networki
Psycholo

> Notice the hanging indent format of all the references. The first line is flush left, and all other lines are indented. To easily achieve this, type all your references using regular double-spacing. Then highlight all citations with your mouse, and while highlighted, press Ctrl+T on the keyboard. This will automatically format the highlighted references for the hanging indent.

Scherer, K. (1997). Co Healthy and unhealthy Internet use. *Journal of nt Development, 38,* 655-665.

Thatcher, chko, G., & Fridjhon, P. (2008). Online flow experience, p matic Internet use and Internet procrastination. *Computers in Human Behavior, 24,* 2236-2254. doi: 10.l016/j.chh.2007.10.008

> The title of the journal is italicized, and so is the volume number, but not the page numbers from the journal article. Also note: There is no issue number in parentheses, even though this information is made available from retrieval databases.

THE INTERNET AND ACADEMICS   13

U.S. Census Bureau. (2007). *Internet use triples in decades, Census Bureau reports*. Retrieved from http://www.census.gov/PressRelease/ www/releases/archives/communication_industries/013849.html

ven though there is only one more reference, it continues onto another ge. Don't try to squeeze erything onto one page.

This is an Internet reference. Notice that a particular person was not the author, so the corporate/governmental author is provided. The date is sometimes tricky; this is the date the item was posted on the Internet (not the date it was retrieved). When the date is not available, use n.d. in parentheses—for example, U.S. Census Bureau. (n.d.). The actual name of the webpage is italicized, followed by the complete URL provided so that the reader can access the same materials you did. Also, the Internet reference does not end in a period, because the URL does not end in a period. Putting a period there would make the URL inaccessible.

THE INTERNET AND ACADEMICS   14

Table 1

Notice that double-spacing continues on this table. Also, the table title is in italics.

Survey Items with Means (M) and Standard Deviations (SD)

Survey Item	M	S D
1. I find that my ~~e~~ of the Internet interferes with my ~~y~~ to get good grades.	2.61	1.05
~~Internet~~ use causes me to ~~my studies.~~	3.58	1.05
~~do~~ you find yourself browsing the Internet for fun when you should be using the Internet for school-related subjects?	1.57	.74
4. How many hours do you use the Internet during an average week (for both academic and entertainment purposes)?	14.96	12.25
5. How many social networking sites do you belong to (i.e., MySpace, Facebook, Twitter)?	1.85	1.24
6. What is your current GPA?	3.28	.54

In an APA-formatted table, there are no vertical lines—only horizontal lines.

Notes. Item 1 and 2 were answered using a Likert-type agreement scale, with 1 = *strongly disagree* to 5 = *strongly agree*. Item 3 was answered using a frequency scale, with 0 = *never* to 3 = *always*. Items 4, 5 and 6 were fill-in-the-blank questions.

The information in the table note is invaluable because it provides a context for the reader to make sense of the means and standard deviations presented in the table.

The primary focus of this book is to help students develop APA-style writing competency. In some chapters in this book, we focused on the basics, such as punctuation, grammar, voice and tone, plagiarism, and the endless details of APA references, citations, tables, and so on. We've given you tips, with examples, on how to conquer each task. However, we have not jumped so deeply into some details, such as how to craft the Introduction section of your research paper, how to adapt rules for APA style and format to a term paper assignment that an instructor might assign, or how to write for the web or prepare for a poster presentation at a conference. There is so much more to develop your scientific writing competency beyond APA style (but that is our major focus here). For other perspectives and different viewpoints about writing in psychology, we suggest you consult any of the following reference works.

Additional Resources on Writing

Beins, B. C., & Beins, A. M. (2008). *Effective writing in psychology: Papers, posters, and presentations.* Malden, MA: Blackwell.

Dunn, D. (2004). *A short guide to writing about psychology.* New York, NY: Longman/ Pearson.

Landrum, R. E. (2008). *Undergraduate writing in psychology: Learning to tell the scientific story.* Washington, DC: American Psychological Association.

Mitchell, M. L., Jolley, J. M., & O'Shea, R. P. (2004). *Writing for psychology: A guide for students.* Belmont, CA: Wadsworth/Thomson Learning.

Rosnow, R. L., & Rosnow, M. (2005). *Writing papers in psychology: A student guide to research papers, essays, proposals, posters, and handouts (with InfoTrac)* (5th ed.). Belmont, CA: Wadsworth/Thomson Learning.

Scott, J. M., Koch, R., Scott, G. M., & Garrison, S. M. (2002). *The psychology student writer's manual* (2nd ed.). Upper Saddle River, NJ: Prentice Hall.

Szuchman, L. T. (2010). *Writing with style: APA style made easy* (5th ed.). Belmont, CA: Wadsworth/Thomson Learning.

Like any complex skill, writing in APA style takes time, practice, and repetition to master. If you want to be good at something, you must practice on a regular basis. If you carefully select classes to avoid writing assignments, you will have difficulty in building your writing confidence because you will not have had multiple opportunities to practice and build that confidence. Also remember this: If you want to make yourself more marketable with your degree, become good at a skill that others avoid. Many of your classmates do not care for writing, nor do they practice it enough; if you can overcome that attitude, embrace the process of writing, and embrace the process of critical thinking that accompanies scientific writing, you will be carving a niche and building a skill set that will serve you well in the workplace, whether you go there directly with your bachelor's degree or attend graduate school and then head to the workplace.

All Together Now

20

How to Avoid the Most Common Mistakes

In Chapter 4, we provided a list of the 20 most common grammatical errors in all types of writing. We end this book with the 21 most common writing errors students make when learning to write in APA style using APA format, plus a list of common instructor pet peeves to keep in mind. Our comments here refer mostly to formal experimental (research) papers, but when instructors say they want a paper prepared in APA format, we strongly suggest you check your work against the list provided here so you can avoid these common mistakes. Attention to detail is often the difference between good and great. Said another way, attention to detail is often the difference between A work and B work. We don't mean to focus on the negative, but we want you to learn the nuances and techniques of writing in APA style, for if you can conquer this, you will have acquired skills that will serve you the remainder of your undergraduate career and beyond.

So before you hand in any assignment that calls for APA format or APA style, we highly recommend that you consult this checklist. We've also included the checklist in an abbreviated format in Appendix B so you can copy it and literally check each item before handing in any APA-style paper. Avoiding these common errors sends good signals to your instructors; you can follow instructions, you can do detailed work, and you know how to translate complex assignments into meaningful scientific writing. The ability to complete this task successfully is a marketable skill. The more you practice, the better you will become, and the faster you'll be able to finish complex writing tasks.

APA Style and Format Checklist

- In an APA-style paper, cite a reference to support a claim about a belief or behavior. If you are going to offer your personal opinion, make sure the source/attribution is clearly identified. To some extent, most instructors assume that anything in the Introduction or Discussion section that does not have a citation is, by default, your personal opinion. If it is your personal opinion consider using the terms "In my opinion" in the text of your paper. If it is not your opinion but you got it from somewhere but did not cite the source you are plagiarizing.

  Incorrect: It is well-known that over half of all marriages end in divorce in the United States.

  Correct: According to the National Survey on Family Growth conducted by the U.S. Department of Health and Human Services (Goodwin, Mosher, & Chandra, 2010), approximately one third of first marriages ended in divorce or separation before reaching the 10th anniversary.

- Use *while* to indicate the passage of time; otherwise, use *although* or *whereas* (see Chapter 4).

  Incorrect: While socioeconomic status is an interesting variable, I did not include it in this study.

  Correct: Although socioeconomic status is an interesting variable, I did not include it in this study.

  Correct: While texting, our participants' driving abilities were significantly impaired.

- Avoid passive voice; strive to write in the active voice, using first-person pronouns (see Chapter 3).

  Incorrect: The study was conducted with groups of participants.

  Correct: I tested participants in groups.

- Avoid common word confusions, such as *than* versus *then* and *effect* versus *affect* (see Chapter 4).

  Incorrect: I hypothesize that men will score higher then women.

  Correct: I hypothesize that men will score higher than women.

  Incorrect: We measured the affect of the independent variable on the dependent variable.

  Correct: We measured the effect of the independent variable on the dependent variable.

- When using APA style, avoid being too colloquial (which means too informal). Avoid sentences such as, "In the next section of this paper, I'm going to talk about . . ." Writing in APA style is not like a conversation.

Incorrect: In the next section of this paper, I will present the major hypotheses.

Correct: I present my hypotheses next.

- When citing references in text, inside parentheses use an ampersand (&) for multiple authors; outside of parentheses, use *and* for multiple authors (see Chapter 7).

Incorrect: The present research is supported by previous literature (Schwartz and Gurung, 2011).

Correct: The present research is supported by previous literature (Schwartz & Gurung, 2011).

Incorrect: Landrum & Gurung (in press) used empirical evidence of learning to write their introduction to psychology textbook.

Correct: Landrum and Gurung (in press) used empirical evidence of learning to write their introduction to psychology textbook.

- Use a semicolon to separate two clauses that could both stand on their own as complete sentences.

Incorrect: The study was complete; then questions.

Correct: The study was complete; participants were free to ask questions.

- Make sure all Latin abbreviations are spelled correctly. The following Latin abbreviations should be used only in parentheses: cf., e.g., etc., i.e., viz., vs. (See Chapter 16 for more details).

Incorrect: We considered many publishers, e.g., McGraw-Hill, Cengage, and Worth.

Correct: We considered many publishers (e.g., McGraw-Hill, Cengage, and Worth).

- Minimize the use of third-person pronouns—*they, their, them*; complete each thought, even if it means being a bit redundant in the sentence. (See Chapter 3 for more information).

Incorrect: We asked them to complete the task and return their booklets over there.

Correct: We asked participants to complete the task and return the booklets at the front of the room.

- Change singular antecedents to plural so you can use plural pronouns instead of *he or she, he/she, him or her,* or *him/her.*

Incorrect: He or she was asked to complete the task and return his or her booklet over there.

Correct: I asked participants to complete the task and return the booklets at the front of the room.

- If you are the only author of a paper, do not refer to *we* or *our*, because you are the only author, refer to *I* or *my* (see Chapter 3 for more). Also, APA style uses *we* and *our* to refer only to the authors of a manuscript, not to people in general.

  Incorrect: Our findings confirm the hypothesis that class attendance positively correlates with exam performance.

  Correct: My findings confirm the hypothesis that class attendance positively correlates with exam performance.

  Incorrect: We need to better understand how our children learn in school.

  Correct: I believe educators need a better understanding of how children learn in school.

- Do not use contractions in APA format.

  Incorrect: The participants weren't allowed to take more than 50 min to complete the survey.

  Correct: The participants were not allowed to take more than 50 min to complete the survey.

- See Chapter 14 for details about changing the spacing using the "paragraph" window in Word.

- Be sure to italicize all statistical symbols and abbreviations (see Chapter 9).

  Incorrect: The age of participants was higher than expected (M = 26.43, SD = 5.44).

  Correct: The age of participants was higher than expected (M = 26.43, SD = 5.44).

- When writing about studies previously conducted in an Introduction section, refer to the studies in past tense, because they were indeed conducted in the past. Note: When writing a proposal for research that you will conduct, write about your proposed research in the future tense, because you have not yet completed the work.

  Incorrect: Aram and Aviram (2009) suggest that frequency of storybook reading relates to a child's language ability.

  Correct: Aram and Aviram (2009) suggested that frequency of storybook reading relates to a child's language ability.

- Be sure to follow the rules for numbers and numerals throughout your APA-style paper (see Chapter 11 for more details).

  Incorrect: Introductory psychology students chose from 2 different textbooks available at the bookstore.

> **Correct:** Introductory psychology students chose from two different textbooks available at the bookstore.
> **Incorrect:** Participants completed the task in forty-five min.
> **Correct:** Participants completed the task in 45 min.

- When citing a paper with three to five authors, include all authors' names for the first citation, and use only the first author's name followed by et al. for all subsequent citations.

  > **First citation:** Schwartz, Landrum, and Gurung (2012) wrote a student-friendly guide to APA style and format.
  > **Second citation:** In their book on APA style and format, Schwartz et al. (2012) included a sample paper for practicing proofreading.

- When citing a study with six or more authors the first time in the text of a paper, use et al. after the first author's name—even on the first citation—with no comma before et al. (see Chapter 7 for more details).

  > **Incorrect:** Taylor, Klein, Lewis, Gruenwald, Gurung, and Updegraff (2000) proposed a new theory of stress called the tend-and-befriend theory.
  > **Correct:** Taylor et al. (2000) proposed a new theory of stress called the tend-and-befriend theory.

- Do not use sophisticated vocabulary to show off. Aim for parsimony; communicate complex ideas in the simplest language possible (see Chapter 3). (In other words, try not to embed SAT- or GRE-type words in your writing unless the word truly fits the context.)

  > **Incorrect:** In preparation for this experiment, a plethora of studies were reviewed.
  > **Correct:** In preparation for this experiment, I reviewed many studies.

- Be careful with the verb *prove*; we don't prove anything in science. You can avoid this issue by discussing whether your findings support your hypothesis or refute your hypothesis rather than proving and disproving your hypothesis.

  > **Incorrect:** My data prove that taller people weigh more than shorter people.
  > **Correct:** My data support the conclusion that taller people tend to weigh more than shorter people.

- Draw appropriate conclusions; correlational data do not allow for cause-and-effect conclusions.

  > **Incorrect:** There was a negative correlation between average number of cigarettes smoked and life span, meaning that cigarette smoking causes an earlier death.
  > **Correct:** There was a negative correlation between average number of cigarettes smoked and life span, meaning results indicated that those who smoked many cigarettes were also those who lived shorter lives.

Be Aware of Professors' Pet Peeves

We all have pet peeves, or certain things that annoy us more and that might not annoy others quite so much. After reading many student papers written by those first learning how to write in APA style, instructors often generate a list of common writing mistakes that they find particularly annoying. Though pet peeves are by nature dependent on the individual in question, through discussions with many colleagues who are grading these papers, we've come across some common items on that list of pet peeves concerning APA style. It is worth your while to learn what those pet peeves are so that you can avoid them.

These are not necessarily in the *PM*, but they are examples of **what to avoid** to strengthen your paper when writing APA-style papers.

- Stating that "research was done." Instead discuss conducting research.
  Incorrect: Researchers did this study to test three hypotheses. (Steaks are done; studies are conducted.)
  Correct: Researchers conducted this study to test three hypotheses.

- Writing that "research reported" rather than "researchers reported." Remember to connect behaviors to humans and not things.
  Incorrect: This study reported that cramming does not aid in long-term retention. (Studies do not report; people or researchers do.)
  Correct: The researchers reported that cramming does not aid in long-term retention.

- Including lists rather than writing the information in paragraph form: Use lists selectively and sparsely; too many lists can appear as an attempt to avoid writing. See Chapter 15 for rules about seriation (the presentation of lists).

- Using too many direct quotations: Minimize your use of direct quotations, especially long direct quotations. Use a direct quotation only when the author has stated something so perfectly that you cannot adequately paraphrase it. Accurate paraphrasing—taking someone else's ideas and translating them into your own words—is a valuable academic skill; practice that skill. If you truly want to make sure you understand something, try to teach that idea to someone else (like your grandmother or grandfather).

Even if your instructor does not require that every assignment be prepared in APA format, the checklist in this chapter will help you avoid common errors; we provide numerous "redirects" that send you to the chapter that contains the information you need to fix the errors. In addition to using our checklist of the common mistakes we've come across when reading student papers, you might find the checklist in Rewey and Valesquez (2009), developed for a journal submission, helpful as well. Their checklist is very comprehensive and covers

APA style for formatting and typing in general as well as rules for different sections of a manuscript. Again, keep in mind that the Rewey and Valesquez checklist focuses on journal submissions and is not necessarily relevant for a paper assignment. As we mentioned earlier in this book, be sure to review the instructions for the specific writing assignment on which you are working.

The good news is that writing in APA style and format becomes easier with practice. Of course, anything feels easier once you have learned the key elements and had a chance to practice. We hope that this book has gone a long way in reducing your fears about APA style. We can also wager that a close reading of this book will do wonders for your writing, how you learn about science, and even the way you think about science. Your three authors had a stimulating time writing this book. We tried to make it fun. We hope you have fun too.

Appendix A

Error List for Chapter 18

Listed below are the errors we can find for the paper included in Chapter 18. If you find any additional errors, send an e-mail to any of the authors. We welcome your e-mails.

Title page

1. A running head is needed on the first page with the words "Running head" included.

2. The title of the paper should not be in bold.

3. The course name, number, and date should be deleted and replaced with the author's affiliation (college or university).

Page 2

4. The running head on pages 2 through 6 of the paper needs to be left justified with the page number right justified.

5. Change "it ts" to "it is." Add a comma after Anacin.

6. The abbreviation for milligrams should be mg.

7. Alphabetize the citations in the parentheses at the end of paragraph 2.

8. At the end of the second paragraph, there should be a period (it should appear after the closing parenthesis around the citations, not before the opening parenthesis).

9. Delete the extra space between the second and third paragraphs.

10. Change the word *which* to *that*.

11. Change the first comma in the last sentence in the third paragraph to a semicolon.

<u>Page 3</u>

12. Add the word *is* before *commonly*. Technical terms should be italicized (e.g., coffee Arabica, Theobroma cocoa). Change the parentheses between *kola nut* and *Cola nitida* to a semicolon. Change the word *completed* to *completely*.

13. Change *while* to *although*. Add a comma after *vary*.

14. The units of time should be abbreviated (min, hr) in several places.

15. Change *half life* to *half-life* where it appears.

16. Remove the hyphen from *caffeine-sensitive*.

17. The word *Others* should not be capitalized.

18. Delete the extra space between the first two paragraphs.

19. Indent the second paragraph.

20. The semicolon should be a period after the word *thoroughly*, and the word *within* should then be capitalized.

21. The year for the Stephenson citation needs to be changed.

22. The third sentence of the third paragraph includes awkward wording (" . . . is the caffeine also works . . .").

<u>Page 4</u>

23. Delete the extra Robertson in the citation at the end of the paragraph.

24. In the first paragraph, *hour* should be abbreviated.

25. This sentence is incomplete: "Although multiple metabolites . . ."

26. Richardson should be Robertson.

27. Change the passive voice in the second paragraph sentence about renal metabolites in the section starting with "have been reported to have been."

28. Alphabetize the citations within parentheses. Add a comma after *urine*.

29. The second full paragraph is right-justified; make the right margin ragged.

30. Again, change Richardson to Robertson.

<u>Page 5</u>

31. Create one sentence out of two for the first two sentences of the last paragraph by changing the period after *mixed* to a colon.

32. Change the word *While* to *Although,* capitalized as the first word of a complete thought after a colon.

33. Add a comma after *muscle,* before *which.* Change the word "are" to "one."

34. Add a comma after *nuclei,* before *which.*

35. Delete the comma after *relief,* before *and why.*

36. Delete the comma after the first author's name and add an ampersand to the citation at the end of the second paragraph.

Page 6

37. Delete the indent for the long quote.

38. Place the period after the block quote, followed by the authors and page (p.) of the quote inside the parentheses.

39. Change *effect* to *affect.*

40. Use an ampersand instead of the word *and* in the citation included in the last paragraph.

41. Avoid using text within parentheses.

42. Move the heading "References" to the next page.

Page 7

43. Use hanging indents for each reference.

44. For references with two authors, add a comma after the initials of the first author, before the ampersand.

45. For a journal article, capitalize only the first word of the title, the first word after a colon, and proper nouns.

46. For the second (Graham) reference, delete the issue number in parentheses.

47. Include only first initials, not full first and middle names.

48. The last reference should end with a period.

Appendix B

APA Style and Format Checklist

___ Cite a reference to support any claim about a belief or behavior.

___ Use *while* to indicate the passage of time; otherwise, use *although* or *whereas.*

___ Avoid passive voice; strive to write in the active voice, using first-person pronouns.

___ Avoid common word confusions, such as *than* versus *then* and *effect* versus *affect.*

___ Avoid being too colloquial or too informal. Writing in APA style is not like a conversation.

___ When citing references in text, inside parentheses use an ampersand (&) for multiple authors; outside of parentheses, use *and* for multiple authors.

___ Use a semicolon to separate two clauses that could both stand on their own as complete sentences.

___ Make sure all Latin abbreviations are spelled correctly.

___ Use the following Latin abbreviations only within parentheses: cf., e.g., etc., i.e., viz., vs.

___ Minimize the use of third-person pronouns—*they, their, them.*

___ Avoid the use of *he or she, he/she, him or her,* and *him/her.*

___ If you are the only author of a paper, do not use *we* or *our,* because you are the only author, instead use *I* or *my.*

___ Do not use contractions.

___ Be sure your paper is double-spaced throughout. (You can change the spacing using the "paragraph" window in Word.)

___ Be sure to italicize all statistical symbols and abbreviations.

___ When writing about studies previously conducted in an Introduction section, refer to the studies in past tense, because they were indeed conducted in the past. Note: When writing a proposal for research that you will conduct, write about your proposed research in the future tense, because you have not yet completed the work.

___ Be sure to follow the rules for numbers and numerals throughout your paper.

___ When citing a study with three to five authors, include all authors' names for the first citation, and use only the first author's name followed by et al. for all subsequent citations.

___ When citing a study with six or more authors, use et al. after the first author's name—even on the first citation—with no comma before et al.

___ Do not use sophisticated vocabulary to show off. Aim for parsimony; communicate complex ideas in the simplest language possible.

___ Be careful with the verb *prove*; we don't prove anything in science. You can avoid this issue by discussing whether your findings support your hypothesis or by refuting your hypothesis.

___ Draw appropriate conclusions; correlation data do not allow for cause-and-effect conclusions.

___ Do not state that "research was done." Instead, discuss conducting research.

___ Write that "researchers reported" rather than "research reported." Remember to connect behaviors to humans, not things.

___ Use lists selectively and sparsely; too many lists can appear as an attempt to avoid writing.

___ Minimize your use of direct quotes, especially long direct quotes.

References

About.com. (n.d.). *Correcting errors in subject-verb agreement.* Retrieved from http://grammar.about.com/od/correctingerrors/a/ASagreement.htm

American Psychological Association. (2010a). *Publication manual of the American Psychological Association* (6th ed.). Washington, DC: Author.

American Psychological Association. (2010b). *Supplemental material: Writing clearly and concisely.* Retrieved from http://www.apastyle.com/manual/supplement/index.aspx

Beins, B. C., & Beins, A. M. (2008). *Effective writing in psychology: Papers, posters, and presentations.* Malden, MA: Blackwell.

BioMedical Editor. (2009). *Writing tips: Active voice and passive voice.* Retrieved from http://www.biomedicaleditor.com/active-voice.html

Bloom, H. S., & Lipsey, M. W. (2004). *Some food for thought about effect size.* Retrieved from http://courses.washington.edu/socw580/readings/Bloom-2004-FoodforThought.pdf

Blue, T. (2000). *It is never could of!* Retrieved from http://grammartips.homestead.com/couldof.html

Brewer, B. W., Scherzer, C. B., Van Raalte, J. L., Petitpas, A. J., & Andersen, M. B. (2001). The elements of (APA) style: A survey of journal editors. *American Psychologist, 56,* 266–267.

Clark, B. (n.d.). *Five grammatical errors that make you look dumb.* Retrieved from http://www.copyblogger.com/5-common-mistakes-that-make-you-look-dumb/

Cohen, J. (1988). *Statistical power analysis for the behavioral sciences.* San Diego, CA: Academic Press.

DailyWritingTips.com. (n.d.). *Passive vs. active voice.* Retrieved from http://www.dailywritingtips.com/passive-vs-active-voice/

Driscoll, D. L. (2009a). *Appropriate pronoun usage.* Retrieved from http://owl.english.purdue.edu/owl/resource/608/06/

Driscoll, D. L. (2009b). *Stereotypes and biased language.* Retrieved from http://owl.english.purdue.edu/owl/resource/608/05/

Dunn, D. (2004). *A short guide to writing about psychology.* New York, NY: Longman/Pearson.

Edelstein, N., Krantz, T., Polaire, M., Sarde, A., & Sweeney, M. (Producers), & Lynch, D. (Director). (2001). *Mulholland Drive* [Motion picture]. United States: Universal Pictures.

EzineArticles.com. (2009a). *Five tips for subject verb agreement.* Retrieved from http://ezinearticles.com/?Five-Tips-For-Subject-Verb-Agreement&id-1107048

EzineArticles.com. (2009b). *Technical writing: A short summary of basic grammar rules in English.* Retrieved from http://ezinearticles.com/?Technical-Writing---A-Short-Summary-of-Basic-Grammar-Rules-In-English&id=1922954

Field, A. (2010). *Discovering statistics using SPSS* (3rd ed.). Thousand Oaks, CA: Sage.

Gaertner-Johnston, L. (2006). Business writing: "That" or "Which"? Retrieved from http://www.businesswritingblog.com/business_writing/2006/01/that_or_which.html

Gilbert, J. (2006). *10 flagrant grammar mistakes that make you look stupid.* Retrieved from http://news.zdnet.co.uk/itmanagement/0,1000000308,39273376,00.htm

Goodwin, P. Y., Mosher, W. D., & Chandra, A. (2010). Marriage and cohabitation in the United States: A statistical portrait based on cycle 6 (2002) of the National Survey of Family Growth (DHHS Pub. No. PHS 2010-1980). *Vital and Health Statistics, 23*(28). Washington, DC: Government Printing Office.

Gottschalk, K., & Hjortshoj, K. (2004). *The elements of teaching writing: A resource for instructors in all disciplines.* Boston, MA: Bedford/St. Martin's Press.

Gurung, R. A. R. (2009, August). Reaping the fruits of SoTL's labor: Using pedagogical research well. In R. A. R. Gurung (Chair), *Advancing pedagogical research (SoTL) in psychology: Models and incentives.* Symposium presented at the 117th Annual Meeting of the American Psychological Association, Toronto, Canada.

Gurung, R. A. R., & Chrouser, C. (2007). Dissecting objectification: Do sexism, athleticism, and provocativeness matter? *Sex Roles, 57,* 91–99.

Gurung, R. A. R., & Johnson, V. (2010). *Do the rich and famous get objectified?* Manuscript under review.

Gurung, R. A. R., Morack, S., & Bloch, H. (2005, June). *Skin sells (and hurts): Objectification and the Miss America 2004 Pageant.* Poster presented at the annual meeting of the American Psychological Society, Los Angeles, CA.

Gurung, R. A. R., & Schwartz, B. M. (2009). *Optimizing teaching and learning: Pedagogical research in practice.* Malden, MA: Blackwell.

Gurung, R. A. R., Weidert, J., & Jeske, A. S. (2010). A closer look at how students study (and if it matters). *Journal of the Scholarship of Teaching and Learning, 10,* 28–33.

Gurung, R. A. R., & Wilson-Doenges, G. (2010). Engaging students in psychology: Building on first-year programs and seminars. In D. S. Dunn, B. C. Beins, M. A. McCarthy, & G. W. Hill IV (Eds.), *Best practices for beginnings and endings in the psychology major* (pp. 93–106). New York, NY: Oxford University Press.

Hegarty, P., Watson, N., Fletcher, L., & McQueen, G. (2010). When gentlemen are first and ladies are last: Effects of gender stereotypes on the order of romantic partners' names. *British Journal of Social Psychology, 11.*

Instructions in regard to preparation of manuscript. (1929). *Psychological Bulletin, 26,* 57–63.

James, W. (1950). *The principles of psychology.* Mineola, NY: Dover. (Original work published 1890)

Johnson, V., & Gurung, R. A. R. (2010). *Diffusing objectification: The role of competence.* Manuscript under review.

Kesler, J. T. (2010). *Problematic internet use and the effect on academic performance.* Unpublished manuscript, Boise State University, Boise, ID.

Kessler, L., & McDonald, D. (2008). *When words collide: A media writer's guide to grammar and style* (7th ed.). Boston, MA: Wadsworth.

Knight, K. L., & Ingersoll, C. D. (1996). Optimizing scholarly communication: 30 tips for writing clearly. *Journal of Athletic Training, 31,* 209–213.

Krieger, S. (2005). *Microsoft Office document designer: Your easy-to-use toolkit and complete how-to source for professional-quality documents.* Redmond, WA: Microsoft Press.

Landrum, R. E. (2008). *Undergraduate writing in psychology: Learning to tell the scientific story.* Washington, DC: American Psychological Association.

Landrum, R. E., & Gurung, R. A. R. (in preparation). *Psychology*. New York, NY: McGraw-Hill Higher Education.

Lorde, A. (1984). Poetry is not a luxury. *Sister outsider*. Berkeley, CA: Crossing Press.

Maddox, M., & Scocco, D. (2009). *Basic English grammar*. Retrieved from http://www.dailywritingtips.com/

Merriam-Webster's collegiate dictionary (11th ed.). (2005). Springfield, MA: Merriam-Webster.

Mitchell, M. L., Jolley, J. M., & O'Shea, R. P. (2004). *Writing for psychology: A guide for students*. Belmont, CA: Wadsworth/Thomson Learning.

Modern Language Association. (2009). *MLA handbook for writers of research papers* (7th ed.). Retrieved from http://www.mla.org/store/CID24/PID363

Nicol, A. A. M., & Pexman, P. M. (2010). *Presenting your findings: A practical guide for creating tables*. Washington, DC: American Psychological Association.

O'Conner, P. T. (1996). *Woe is I: The grammarphobe's guide to better English in plain English*. New York, NY: Riverhead Books.

O'Conner, P. T. (1999). *Words fail me: What everyone who writes should know about writing*. New York, NY: Harcourt Brace.

O'Neil, D. (2006). *Ethnicity and race: Overview*. Retrieved from http://anthro.palomar.edu/ethnicity/ethnic_1.htm

Pashler, H., McDaniel, M., Rohrer, D., & Bjork, R. (2008). Learning styles: Concepts and evidence. *Psychological Science in the Public Interest, 9*, 105–119. doi:10.1111/j.1539-6053.2009.01038.x

PlainLanguage.gov. (n.d.). *Writing tip: Use active, not passive sentences*. Retrieved from http://www.plainlanguage.gov/howto/quickreference/dash/dashactive.cfm

Prestwich, A., Perugini, M., & Hurling, R. (2010). Can implementation intentions and text messages promote brisk walking? A randomized trial. *Health Psychology, 29,* 40–49. doi:10.1037/a0016993

Reid, J. (1984). *Perceptual learning-style preference questionnaire*. Retrieved from http://lookingahead.heinle.com/filing/l-styles.htm

Rewey, K. L., & Valesquez, T. L. (2009). Presubmission checklist for the *Publication Manual of the American Psychological Association* (6th ed.). *Psi Chi Journal of Undergraduate Research, 14*, 133–136.

Rosnow, R. L., & Rosnow, M. (2005). *Writing papers in psychology: A student guide to research papers, essays, proposals, posters, and handouts (with InfoTrac)* (5th ed.). Belmont, CA: Wadsworth/Thomson Learning.

Schwartz, B. M., & Gurung, R. A. R. (Eds.). (2011). *Picking, choosing, and using pedagogy: An empirical guide*. Washington, DC: American Psychological Association.

Schwartz, B. M., Landrum, R. E., & Gurung, R. A. R. (2012). *An easyguide to APA style*. Thousand Oaks, CA: Sage.

Scott, J. M., Koch, R., Scott, G. M., & Garrison, S. M. (2002). *The psychology student writer's manual* (2nd ed.). Upper Saddle River, NJ: Prentice Hall.

Sic. (2003). *Merriam-Webster's 11th new collegiate dictionary*. Springfield, MA: Merriam-Webster.

Strunk, W., Jr., & White, E. B. (1979). *The elements of style* (3rd ed.). New York, NY: Macmillan.

Szuchman, L. T. (2005). *Writing with style: APA style made easy* (3rd ed.). Belmont, CA: Wadsworth/Thomson Learning.

Todd, J., & Todd, S. (Producers), & Nolan, C. (Director). (2000). *Memento* [Motion picture]. Universal City, CA: Summit Entertainment.

Truss, L. (2003). *Eats, shoots & leaves: The zero tolerance approach to punctuation*. New York, NY: Gotham Books/Penguin.

Ulrich, B. (2005). Eliminating biased language: A goal for everyone. *Nephrology Nursing Journal, 32,* 9.

U.S. Census Bureau. (2008). *Racial and ethnic classifications used in Census 2000 and beyond.* Retrieved from http://www.census.gov/propulation/socdemo/race/racefactcb.html

VandenBos, G. R. (Ed.). (2007). *APA dictionary of psychology.* Washington, DC: American Psychological Association.

Vipond, D. (1993). *Writing and psychology: Understanding writing and its teaching from the perspective of composition studies.* Westport, CT: Praeger.

Wagner, J., Lawrick, E., Angeli, E., Moore, K., Anderson, M., & Soderlund, L. (2009). *APA stylistics: Avoiding bias.* Retrieved from http://owl.english.purdue.edu/owl/resource/560/14/

Webster's third new international dictionary of the English language unabridged. (2002). Springfield, MA: Merriam-Webster.

Wilson, J. H., Stadler, J. R., Schwartz, B. M., & Goff, D. M. (2009). Touching your students: The impact of a handshake on the first day of class. *Journal of the Scholarship of Teaching and Learning, 9,* 108–117. Retrieved from http://academics.georgiasouthern.edu/ijsotl/v4n1.html

Index

SAGE Research Methods Online

The essential tool for researchers